THE WORKING WOMAN'S HANDBOOK

THE
WORKING WOMAN'S
HANDBOOK

Ideas, Insights, and Inspiration
for a Successful Creative Career

Phoebe Lovatt

PRESTEL
Munich · London · New York

CONTENTS

INTRO

THE LEGWORK

WORK IT!

MAKE IT WORK

WORK WELL

WORKING ON 100

OUTRO

INTRO

⊙

A USER'S GUIDE

Welcome to *The Working Woman's Handbook*—a book created to provide all the ideas, insights, and inspiration you need for your successful creative career.

If you've picked up this book, it's likely that work is important to you, and that you're determined to do it as effectively and as joyfully as possible. Props! Most of us will spend the majority of our waking lives at work. It makes sense that we should dedicate some time to learning how to do it well.

Why? Because work is essential. Work is enriching. Work can be an immense source of pleasure. But work is work for a reason: It takes effort, persistence, and concentration. We live in an age when we have more options of where and how to work than ever before (this is brilliant), but also one in which personal identity corresponds almost inextricably with societal standards of career success (not so fun). People who have "figured out" work—the self-made entrepreneurs, the wildly successful creative freelancers, the Internet startup stars—have become the icons of our time.

But the way that we work is changing. The Internet happened, so how could it not? Many of us now have the tools to create, share, and promote our ideas with ease. The global economic meltdown has killed off the idea of job security and given us the impetus to find work we truly love.

For ambitious women who want to live and work on our own terms, this is all pretty thrilling … but it can be confusing as well. We're empowered to direct our careers in a host of new and exciting directions, but the logistics of this operation can seem hazy, at best. Too many women are still being held back by a lack of practical information, guidance, support, and (crucially) confidence. It's time for that to end.

It's vital that we learn about how to work well, to ensure that it doesn't consume a disproportionate amount of our identities, thoughts, and lives. Work is important not just because it provides the financial means to enjoy nice food, travel, and good times with good people, but also because feeling positive about work allows you to live a better life, all-round.

The Working Woman's Handbook is split into five sections, each intended to help you with an aspect of your working life, including, but not limited to: how and where to start; planning your work; money matters; evolving your career; and balancing your hustle with your health. You can progress through them methodically or skip straight to the section you need most.

Whether you're just starting out or have found yourself stuck in a rut, this book will provide the information and inspiration you need to flourish in your creative career. (A quick side note on the term "creative" as I've used it here: I believe that all human beings are creative, especially those seeking to forge their own paths in life. Even if you don't intend to make money from the arts, you can still have a creative career. Cool? Cool.)

Throughout the book, you'll also find interviews with successful women who are really good at what they do, sharing insights on how they do it. I've also included lots of tips, worksheets, and infographics in each section. Write directly onto the pages, or scan and print copies for yourself and your friends. There's power in putting pen to paper: this much I believe to be true.

However you choose to use it, I hope this book helps you to build a career you love, make work you're truly proud of, and have a huge amount of fun along the way.

Thanks for reading,
Phoebe Lovatt

MY WORKING LIFE—SO FAR

My working life began when I was a precocious 13-year-old who somehow managed to talk her way into an internship at the London-based teen magazine *Elle Girl*. Don't ask what motivated me to enter the working world at such a tender age, or how I managed to blag it: I can't really account for either. What I do remember is that, whether I was knee-deep in clothing samples in the fashion cupboard or making nine cups of tea at a time for the Features team, I loved being in an environment full of brilliant, creative people.

From that point onwards, I interned during every summer break and often at Easter, too, working my way across a dozen music and style publications, and then traveling to do the same in New York and Miami during my gap year. By the time I was at university in London, a British music magazine entrusted me to actually *write* a piece on a then-unknown band called The xx. Everything about the process—but especially the interview itself—was exciting to me. I realized that getting into the minds of talented people was something I wanted to do, time and time again.

Aside from a one-year stint working as a content editor for a hospitality group, I've worked for myself ever since: mostly as a journalist and editor, and more recently as a moderator, presenter, and independent business owner. I don't come from a wealthy family, but my parents were always self-employed and somehow managed to make ends meet. From them, I learned how to live on an unstable freelance budget by building as many sources of regular income as possible, working for the same clients over and over, and, crucially, staying realistic in my material wants and needs. A lot of my ability to support myself as a freelancer almost as soon as I graduated came from the legwork I did early on. Through the internships and side hustles I'd pursued, I'd made enough contacts to go it alone from the get-go.

In 2012, I made the decision to move to Los Angeles by myself, leaving behind my hometown—and my hometown crew—in the process. There were lots of things that were hard about starting life in a new city, but being away from my network of supportive, inspiring female friends was probably the hardest. After one too many days feeling lonely and isolated, I decided to start a group to connect women in the creative industries worldwide. I wanted it to be a place where likeminded women could go to meet, work, and maybe have a cocktail together. And so The Working Women's Club (aka The WW Club) was born, named with a tongue-in-cheek nod to the traditional working men's clubs that once existed across the UK.

Since launching The WW Club's first pop-up coworking and events space in downtown LA in January 2015, I've hosted meetups, conversation panels, work parties, wellness sessions, workshops, and dinner parties everywhere from Paris to Brooklyn to Taipei. Through it all, I've met hundreds of insightful women (and hopefully enabled hundreds more to meet each other through our events and membership program). I've also interviewed many incredible working women around the world, extracting every bit of useful information possible and putting it out via The WW Club's blog and newsletters, and my podcast, *Make It Work*.

One of my personal reasons for starting The WW Club was to give myself a platform to launch my moderating and speaking career. And guess what? It worked. As people began to see me lead thought-provoking panel discussions and stand up to welcome large groups of guests to my events, they started booking me to do the same for their brands and businesses—all because I gave myself the license to prove that I could do it. I didn't wait around for someone to give me permission to try something new, and I don't recommend that you should, either!

I've gleaned many golden nuggets of wisdom and advice during the course of my own career, ultimately learning that there's no reason why you can't create a job and life that you really like. All it takes is some practical skills, a solid support network, and a few bright ideas from people who have worked it out (or at least some of it; no one has everything figured out, despite what their Instagram feed might suggest). I've learned to use my enthusiasms and interests as the ultimate career guide. And when I reach a plateau, I try my very best to carve out time for a passion project that is totally unrelated to work … and yet somehow always leads to my next big move?! Go figure.

In *The Working Woman's Handbook*, I've brought together some of the most inspiring interviews and useful information I've picked up since I joined the world of work. If you're just starting out, or maybe stuck in a rut along the way, I hope that this will help you to create a career—and life—you love.

A MANIFESTO

THE NEW RULES OF WORK

JUST START
Where you are. With what you have.

KEEP IT SIMPLE
Quality over quantity.

MAKE STUFF
Stay connected to your creativity at all times.

FEED YOUR MIND
You get out what you put in.

TELL A STORY
Use words and images wisely.

NOTHING GOOD COMES EASY
Let go of instant gratification.

BE HERE NOW
Presence over productivity.

BEST HEALTH IS BEST PRACTICE
A healthy mind + body = a healthy career.

FIND YOUR TEAM
No woman is an island.

YOU ARE NOT YOUR JOB
Don't reduce your life to your title.

IT WILL GET DONE
One day at a time. One task at a time.

LIVE IN REAL LIFE
Step away from the screen sometimes.

KNOW YOUR WORTH
Take pride. Create value.
Don't undersell your work (or yourself).

CHOOSE CLARITY
It's a decision like any other.

HAVE FUN!
Find your flow state, and stay in it.

FIND A WAY TO ENJOY THE EVERYDAY
Today is all we have.

THE
LEGWORK

HOW AND WHERE TO START

Getting started. Isn't that the easy bit?

Yeah, right.

Sometimes, it feels as though the most impossible part of the entire puzzle is figuring out which piece to pick up first. We have more freedom to shape our careers now than at any other point in history, and with that comes the infamous paradox of choice: the ironic truth that, the more options we have, the harder it is to select any option at all.

In our globalized, hyper-connected world, we're overwhelmed by career anxiety, often riddled with self-doubt, and frequently paralyzed by fear of doing it all wrong. Or perhaps we know exactly what we want to do, but we have no idea *how*: What to do first? Who to ask? Where, and when, and, well … *why*?

This chapter is the equivalent of your first cup of coffee of the day: It will help you to feel as though you can do just about anything. And you can. You just need a goal, a method, and a bit of inspiration.

Let's get started, shall we?

START WHERE YOU ARE
Ways to Gain Insight and Get Going

PAY ATTENTION TO YOUR ATTENTION

Maybe you've just graduated from university. Maybe you're three years into your career. Maybe you feel lost, uninspired, or just confused. You want to build a working life you love but can't quite figure out how.

It's not hard to locate the source of the confusion: The pressure to "find your passion" is one of the most misguided and disorienting myths of the modern working world. So, here's an idea: Instead of looking for the things you *might* enjoy in the future, pay attention to the things that command your attention right now.

> Your current interests provide important clues. What searches do you plug into Google, over and over? What type of clickbait lures you in? What kind of Instagram accounts do you love to scroll?

PICK YOUR BATTLES

Next, think about the kinds of challenge you like to take on, and how you like to approach them. This could be anything as mundane as organizing your underwear drawer or as ambitious as building a piece of furniture from scratch. Maybe you like the logistical conundrum of producing a large-scale event. Perhaps you like to beautify spaces, objects, or faces.

> Work is work for a reason: It requires mental or physical effort. What sort of effort do you want to expend, and how?

THINK ABOUT FLOW

You might be familiar with the concept of "flow," which refers to the sensation of being completely absorbed in an activity to the point where you lose track of time. This is the optimum creative state: the one where you're totally engaged in what you're doing. Any job that involves time spent in this state—even if only for brief periods—is likely to be one that you'll enjoy a lot. This is good because if you enjoy it a lot, you'll probably get really good at it.

> What types of activities truly engage you? When do you feel most absorbed in what you're doing?

GETTING "PAID"

Finally, think about the type of rewards system that might work for you. For some people, making lots of money is an essential way to feel valued. Others are satisfied with the idea of creating beautiful objects, or helping others. Consider what makes you feel as though your efforts have been worthwhile and, conversely, what fails to bring you much satisfaction.

> What does work mean to you, and how do you want to be paid for it? When did you last feel really rewarded for your work, and why?

MAKE STUFF

Are you already making stuff? Take a minute to contemplate the past five things you created from scratch. Maybe you love to put together beautiful plates of food when you get home from your desk job, or perhaps you update a literary blog just for fun. Anything you're self-motivated to make without being told to could provide the key to your future career.

> What do you create, just for the love of doing it?

EXERCISE 1:
A Guide to Getting Started

ATTENTION
What topics never fail to catch
your eye? What do you like to
read about and research?

_____

_____

_____

_____

CHALLENGES
What kinds of problems do you
like to tackle and solve?

_____

_____

_____

_____

FLOW
Think of three times you got
lost in the moment. What were
you up to?

_____

_____

_____

_____

VALUE
Think of three instances when
you felt valued and helpful.
What form did your reward take?

_____

_____

_____

_____

KNOWLEDGE
List three areas you know a
fair amount about (and would
like to learn a lot more).

_____

_____

_____

_____

CREATIONS
What were the last three things
you made that satisfied you?

_____

_____

_____

_____

EXERCISE 1: CONTINUED

PATTERNS

What's coming up here?
Make some notes on themes that have popped out.

THREE INITIAL IDEAS

Take the information above and use it to generate three ideas
for creative projects you could make work.

1

2

3

WORK STYLES + LIFESTYLES
Five Big Questions to Ask Yourself
Before You Start

WHAT DOES "THE GOOD LIFE" MEAN TO YOU?

Forget your job for a second. What kind of *life* do you really want? This might sound like a self-indulgent question, but it's important to consider the full picture if you're hoping to build a career you love.

Work is just one aspect of a happy life, so take some time to really think about what role you want it to play in yours. In today's culture, entrepreneurship is often treated as the highest rung of career status, but it's definitely not for everyone. Equally, the stability of a 9-to-5 job would drive some people to madness. Know yourself, and be realistic about what you want and need.

> TIP
>
> Think back to the last time you woke up feeling truly excited to tackle the day's work. What were you doing? Whom were you doing it with? At what point did you clock off to go spend time with family and friends?

WHAT'S REALLY WORTH IT?

Your values are your life's priorities. Everyone's differ and change, but thinking about what truly matters to you *today* will help you take action in both the short and the long term. *Don't* worry about what you might care about in 10 years. *Do* ensure that you're putting your time into the things you truly care about now.

> TIP
>
> Write a list that comprises all the elements that constitute your vision of a happy life. This could be anything from "family" to "financial success." Then, put these values in order, and think about how your current life compares. Are you currently investing your energy into the areas that bring you the most satisfaction? If not, how can you rearrange things to do so?

MAINTAIN THE CASH FLOW

It's super important to pursue work that might bring you personal satisfaction, but you also have to consider what value that work might have in the marketplace. To make your passion into your career, you're going to have to identify who exactly is going to pay you to do so. Will it be individual clients or customers? Agencies? Brands or businesses? Government or civic institutions?

> TIP
>
> Write out your key income sources over the past 12 months. How much did each client, product, or service bring in? How can you develop those relationships or offerings to continue cash flow?
>
> Now, list five ways you could potentially bring in income over the next 12 months. How will you secure these commissions or profits? How much could you potentially make from each project or client?

WHAT DO YOU WANT TO GET GOOD AT?

Wherever you're at in your life, you've already developed skills in one key area—or maybe more. How can you develop these skills into a niche? What are you excited to develop and study as part of your professional USP (Unique Selling Point)?

> TIP
>
> Think about the last five things you were asked to do, either as paid work or as a favor to friends. What's the common denominator of these tasks? What are you known for being good at? Do you want to get even better?

WHERE ARE YOU GOING?

We live in rapidly changing times shaped by a constant stream of technological innovations. Many of us have entered the working world in an era of financial and political upheaval; a world in which work and gender are undergoing transformative change. There's no way of knowing what life will throw at you, but you should plan for the future you've no doubt mapped out in your mind.

> TIP
>
> Picture yourself in three years. What are the key components of your life?
>
> Now take that vision and write out the key steps you'll need to take to get there. Use the three major headings of:
>
> WORK, RELATIONSHIPS, WELLBEING

EXERCISE 2:
Employed, Freelance, or Entrepreneur?

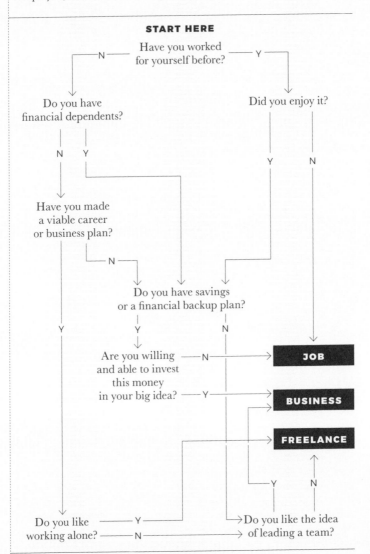

START HERE

Have you worked for yourself before?

Do you have financial dependents?

Did you enjoy it?

Have you made a viable career or business plan?

Do you have savings or a financial backup plan?

Are you willing and able to invest this money in your big idea?

JOB

BUSINESS

FREELANCE

Do you like working alone?

Do you like the idea of leading a team?

GET YOUR MIND RIGHT
Essential Foundations for Starting
(and Staying) Strong

BUILD CONFIDENCE AS IF YOUR JOB DEPENDS ON IT

Call it cultural conditioning. Call it Imposter Syndrome. Call it The Insane Pressure of Being a Woman in the 21st Century. Call it whatever you like. But know that low self-confidence is the greatest enemy of professional progress and that if you don't believe you're capable of establishing the career you want, it's unlikely that you ever will.

Confidence comes from two sources: doing and believing. The doing part is about setting goals and executing them—even if it's not in the exact way you'd envisioned—and therefore bolstering your self-belief. The believing part is less tangible, and harder to build. It comes from creating an inner source of strength that keeps you motivated when things go wrong, or seem as if they're about to. Confidence, like proper email etiquette and successful pitching, is a professional skill you must develop. Devote time to building this skill, just like any other.

> **TIP**
>
> Identify the areas where you feel lacking in confidence and come up with practical solutions for building yourself up. For example, if money is a weak spot, do some reading, create a budget, and add a small amount of cash to your savings account. Being proactive will empower you!

ACCEPT THAT CLARITY IS A CHOICE

Few things are more disorienting than feeling that you lack clarity. We all want to operate with focus and purpose: an idea that this is all adding up to something that makes sense. Our late teens and twenties in particular can seem like an endlessly confusing time, in which all the anchors of childhood are lost and the stabilizers of adulthood have yet to be established. Add in a fickle economy and a mind-warping social media culture and it's no wonder we all feel a bit lost.

Regain your sense of calm by accepting that clarity is not a state of mind that magically descends upon you, but rather a mindset you can choose to adopt. It arises when you make decisions about what you want, and how you're going to get it. It comes from having faith in your own gut instinct. It takes root when you accept that there is no way to know exactly what the "best" way of doing things might be: There's only the choice you can make with the information you have right now.

Alleviate some of that stress by trying to adopt a more playful approach to your work. Treat each project or plan as an experiment: You can control the elements of the experiment, but there's no totally accurate way to predict the results. One thing that is certain is that you'll never know until you try. So try. If it doesn't work out, you've learned something, and you're now better equipped to create a desirable outcome the next time around.

TIP

Your mental and physical health play a huge part in your ability to feel clear-headed and focused. Be mindful of excessive alcohol and caffeine intake, meditate in any way that works for you (yoga, walking), and make sure you're getting enough sleep and exercise. For more tips on feeling good, turn to page 141.

TIP

Every time you have an idea, or get stuck on a problem, write a list of 10 ways you could tackle that particular situation. Forcing yourself to come up with numerous different approaches to the same issue will help to unblock your thinking and yield more imaginative solutions.

TREAT LIFE AS AN EXPERIMENT

One way to become more comfortable with the decision-making process that leads to clarity is by loosening the reins. When it comes to your work (especially when you're self-employed), it's easy to be paralyzed by a fear that you're working on the wrong things, or doing them in the wrong way.

TAKE ACTION, ALWAYS

As a creative person, you probably have tons of ideas. So many ideas, in fact, that you may well get overwhelmed by trying to decide which ones you should act on, and which you should bank for another day. You might even have so many ideas that you forget about the ones you have, or quickly override existing projects when you hit a wall and something more exciting comes along.

THE LEGWORK

Don't do that! Inaction ultimately breeds self-doubt. Every time you fail to bring an idea to fruition (even if it's exactly as you'd envisioned), you'll lose a little bit of faith in your ability to honor your own word.

TIP

Use the planner on page 28 to plot your goals, then post them somewhere you'll see them every day. Work with schedules to ensure that you execute your ideas in a timely fashion, and resist the urge to add new projects until you've found a way to bring your current ideas to life.

TIP

List of all your achievements in the past 3, 6, or 12 months. Seeing all the things you've made happen in black and white will give you the motivation you need to keep going.

What's going well? What made you money? What did you enjoy? And—crucially—how can you do more of all of the above?

CELEBRATE YOUR SUCCESSES

Ambitious people rarely stop to smell the roses, but marking your achievements is essential to staying inspired in the long run. Don't crack open the champagne every time you publish a blog post, but do make time to think about the things that have gone right (just as you make time to assess what has gone wrong!). If you can't get your head around the idea of "patting yourself on the back," think of it as a useful feedback session from you to you.

MAKE A DIGITAL MOODBOARD

Having your goals where you can see them is essential to staying motivated and on track. It's important to elucidate your thoughts by writing everything out clearly (see Exercise 3), but visuals are important, too. On the first day of each month, think about the vibes you want to channel for the days ahead, pull a load of inspiring images and quotes into a Google Drawings file, and then set that image as your desktop background. Every time you lose track of where you're at, minimize whatever tabs you have open and check in with your digital moodboard. It's easy, fun, and environmentally friendly. Give it a try.

EXERCISE 3:
A Clear Goal-Setting Guide

THE BIG IDEA
Summarize your focus for the year in five words or less. This should be a broad statement that can be used as a mantra, i.e., "Empower women with practical information."

3 GOALS FOR THE YEAR

1. PROFESSIONAL (SOMETHING CAREER-RELATED)

2. PERSONAL (SOMETHING THAT HAS NOTHING TO DO WITH WORK)

3. HABITUAL (SOMETHING YOU WANT TO DO/NOT DO IN YOUR DAILY LIFE)

5 STEPS TO TAKE EACH QUARTER THAT ENABLE YOU TO ACHIEVE THESE GOALS

Q1	Q2	Q3	Q4
1	1	1	1
2	2	2	2
3	3	3	3
4	4	4	4
5	5	5	5

EXERCISE 3: CONTINUED

MONTHLY

Break down your month into weeks and pull to-dos into a
weekly schedule.

WEEK 1	WEEK 2	WEEK 3	WEEK 4
TO-DO	TO-DO	TO-DO	TO-DO

DAILY

List three things that will take you towards your goal each day.

1

2

3

Elaine Welteroth

EDITOR OF *TEEN VOGUE*

The dynamic magazine editor on her fear of "failure to launch," our obligation for self-actualization, and why Gen Z will save us all

HOMETOWN
Newark, CA

CURRENT LOCATION
Brooklyn, NY

EDUCATION
BA in Media/Communications with a minor in Journalism—California State University, Sacramento

EXPERIENCE
• Beauty & Style Editor, *Ebony* magazine
• Senior Beauty Editor, *Glamour* magazine
• Beauty & Health Director, *Teen Vogue* magazine

WHAT KIND OF KID WAS ELAINE? Oh, man, I was energetic, opinionated, fun-loving, creative, and probably a pain in the ass! But no—I was very just interested in everything. I definitely thrived on being busy and being a big social butterfly. In school, I did every single sport. I was in the school choir. I was the Junior and Senior class president. I was just very *busy* [laughs].

I GREW UP IN THE BAY AREA IN A VERY LIBERAL FAMILY. They were pretty much like: "No matter what you want to do, we're going to support you and love you." I'm the first person in my family to graduate from college, so I felt like I had to figure out a lot of the professional climb on my own.

I WOULD BE THE KID WHO WOULD STAY UP UNTIL 3 O'CLOCK IN THE MORNING WITH A FLASHLIGHT IN MY ROOM, PRETENDING TO BE SLEEPING BUT REALLY PUTTING TOGETHER LITTLE COLLAGES. I *loved* collages, I *loved* magazines. It's funny how those things that you spent your time obsessing over as a kid totally translate into a real-life passion that you can get paid for as an adult.

AT EVERY PARTY IN COLLEGE, I WAS THE PERSON WHO WAS IN A CORNER WITH SOMEONE I'D FIND, WHO WOULD TELL ME THEIR LIFE STORY. By the end we'd be hugging and crying, and having a therapy session. My mum always calls me "Little Baba Wawa," as in Barbara Walters, because I am always extracting all the facts from someone on their life. That's just the way I enjoy socializing! To this day that is the best part of my job—interviewing people.

MY NUMBER ONE PIECE OF ADVICE IS: *DON'T FOLLOW THAT BOY TO COLLEGE!* I chose my college for the absolute worst reason, which was to go wherever my high-school sweetheart was going. Ultimately, I don't think it was the best school choice for me, but I made the best of it. The experience taught me that: *Holy shit, it's really on you to figure out how to make your dreams come true.* No counselor is going to carve out that path for you, especially if you want to work in a creative industry.

MY WORST FEAR WAS BEING A FAILURE TO LAUNCH. I was like: "I have to figure out how to be great." As a first step, during my college winter intercession, I went to LA for an entertainment PR internship. While I was down there, I ended up getting this cool on-camera opportunity to interview musicians. That was the first time I remember tasting the intersection of vision and faith, and realizing that *that's* when the magic of life takes hold of you. I got addicted to that feeling.

MY NEXT GOAL WAS NEW YORK. I moved across the country for a summer internship in advertising. To be honest,

I hated it! But it was a great experience because it exposed me to new possibilities. I remember thinking, "Well, I hate doing this, but I love this New York thing. And if I can make it in New York doing something I don't love, why don't I try to make it to New York for something I do love?"

I ACCIDENTALLY TOOK TOO MANY CREDITS FOR A FEW SEMESTERS, SO I ENDED UP GRADUATING EARLIER THAN I'D EXPECTED. That sent me into this anxiety-stricken period of my life, where I felt an urgency to figure my life out. I remember going home and rabidly looking through magazines, looking for inspiration to hit me. I picked up *Ebony* magazine and Alicia Keys was on the cover wearing a beautiful red gown. I read the cover story, and something told me to Google the author—I'd never done that before in my life—but something told me to, so I did. This woman's name was Harriette Cole.

[HARRIETTE] HAD ESSENTIALLY CREATED A BRAND FOR HERSELF. I read about how she leveraged a really successful career as a fashion editor at *Essence*, then became Editor in Chief of *Ebony* magazine. She parlayed that into an on-air role as a TV personality, and had a syndicated radio show and became a best-selling author. At the time, in my eyes, that was revolutionary. The only other person I knew of who'd done that was Oprah. This was all pre-social media where everyone has a "personal brand" now.

A LIGHTBULB WENT OFF INSIDE OF ME. I was like: *I want to be like this woman.* So I wrote her a letter that night, sent it snail mail, and followed up like *crazy.* I found the phone number for her office, and I called to say I would love to have 10 minutes to talk to Harriette. They kept saying, "No, she's not available," and I would say, "What if I come to New York and bring her coffee?" At some point, they must have been like, "Harriette better get on the phone with this crazy girl before she shows up at our office."

EVENTUALLY I LOCKED IN A PHONE CALL. It was supposed to be just 15 minutes but there was so much synergy that we ended up on the line for 45 minutes. At the end of the call, I said, "If there's ever an opportunity to work with you,

We all have an obligation to self-actualize. That is your singular goal on this planet: If you feel like you are meant to be here for a certain reason, you have to follow that. No boy can get in the way; no sexy job title that you're not excited about; no amount of money can keep you from that pursuit.

please keep me in mind." We hung up, and I thought, "She's definitely going to forget about me." But in a magical turn of events, four months later, Harriette offered me a role at *Ebony*. I moved to NYC to start as her intern and then—in another bold-ass move that I would not recommend!—the three-month internship ended and I was still there, so I changed my title in my email signature to Production Assistant! Somehow I got away with that [laughs]. I worked my way up from there, and eventually I started the Beauty and Style department at *Ebony*. I learned so much through those years that has helped me throughout my entire career. After that, I went to Condé Nast to work at *Glamour* magazine for a year as Senior Beauty Editor.

THEN, AT 25, I WAS OFFERED THE GAME-CHANGING ROLE OF MY CAREER: BEAUTY AND HEALTH DIRECTOR AT *TEEN VOGUE*. I was in that role for about four years and I wore a lot of different hats. I ended up taking on cover stories when I could, and I wrote some features. I have to give a lot of credit to Amy Astley, who was the founding Editor in Chief, because she gave all of us the opportunity to have our voices heard. She wasn't a micromanager: She was someone who allowed you to spread your wings and really fly.

WHEN ANNA [WINTOUR] CALLED ME INTO HER OFFICE TO OFFER ME THE POSITION OF EDITOR OF *TEEN VOGUE*, IT WAS A HUGE HONOR. It also felt like a very seamless transition. I didn't really feel the need to make a huge statement about the direction of the magazine when I took the job: Internally, we had been working together as a team to shift what *Teen Vogue* could mean to our audience. There was evolution underway—I really wanted to go beyond beauty and fashion to be more intentional about sending messages of empowerment and telling stories that would provoke more compelling political conversations.

I WORK REALLY CLOSELY WITH OUR DIGITAL EDITORIAL DIRECTOR AND CREATIVE DIRECTOR. We call ourselves the dream team; we share the same vision of being a progressive voice for young, conscious people. We're all about using fashion and beauty as lenses to have larger conversations about the importance of diversity, empowerment, and self-expression—and we aren't afraid to dive into the political issues that matter to young people. It's our responsibility. And we don't take that lightly.

GEN Z IS GOING TO SAVE ALL OF US. We have a very woke team. I have to say that, and I have to shout out our digital team, because they're leading the charge in the political conversation that *Teen Vogue* is getting a lot of credit for right now. I think that it's a combination of our personal passions meeting the right political climate, and these incredible opportunities to lead this very important brand for young people.

THE YOUTH HAVE ALWAYS BEEN ON THE RIGHT SIDE OF HISTORY. I feel immensely fortunate to help lead the charge in capturing the consciousness of young people today. I see myself, and I see *Teen Vogue* as a conduit for those voices that are already doing, thinking, saying the things the world needs to hear more of right now. We are a platform for them, we're here to amplify their voices. Our readers and the young thought leaders that we lend our pages to are a consistent source of hope to me.

WHAT ADVICE WOULD I GIVE MY 18-YEAR-OLD SELF?
Go fearlessly in the direction of your dream. I think a lot about that period of just feeling really hopeless about the future. Fear could easily have kept me from sending that letter out to Harriette and incessantly following up, but ultimately those actions formed the tipping point that launched me into the seat I'm in right now.

WE ALL HAVE AN OBLIGATION TO SELF-ACTUALIZE.
That is your singular goal on this planet: If you feel like you are meant to be here for a certain reason, you *have* to follow that. No boy can get in the way; no sexy job title that you're not excited about; no amount of money can keep you from that pursuit. When you feel that passion inside of you, you have to follow it. You just *have* to.

Sandy Liang

DESIGNER, SANDY LIANG

The clothing designer and native New Yorker on the importance of a good coat, living life outside the bubble, and creating clothes that make people smile

HOMETOWN
New York, NY

EDUCATION
BFA in Fashion Design—Parsons School of Design, NY

CURRENT LOCATION
New York, NY

EXPERIENCE
• Press internship, 3.1 Phillip Lim
• Design internship, Opening Ceremony
• Design internship, Richard Chai

I'M A FASHION DESIGNER, BUT I DON'T REALLY SEE MYSELF AS ONE. I present when I have to present, I do sales when I have to do sales, but I just make the clothes. A lot of that has to do with the fact that I'm not a big company, where we have market research to figure out what people want to buy. It's really just me making what I want to wear right now; what my friends want to wear right now (or next season, rather).

I DID MY FIRST COLLECTION WHEN I WAS 22. I had just graduated from fashion school and my dad suggested that I should get a job and gain some experience for at least a couple of years before even thinking about doing my own thing. But I was so stubborn, and I was high off this energy. I really believed in myself.

I SAID TO MY DAD, "I'M GOING TO FUCK UP SO MANY TIMES AND MAKE SO MANY MISTAKES, ANYWAY. WHY CAN'T I DO IT NOW?" Start everything now, and just figure it out along the way. There's never going to be a right time to start something like this, right?

THERE'S NEVER A START POINT OR END POINT TO THE INSPIRATION FOR THE SEASON. It has a lot to do with my personal life and whatever I am going through at that time.

I LIKE THINGS WITH DUALITY. I'm really, really into old Range Rovers, pre-2001 models: I like how they're regal and associated with the English countryside, but at the same time, American hip-hop culture has made them into this whole other *thing*. They're cool because they're meant to get dirty, they're not meant to look pretty and polished.

I THINK THAT APPLIES TO MY CLOTHES AS WELL. I don't think they should ever be too polished. That's just not my girl, that's just not me.

HOW DID I START MY LABEL? First off, by getting all the legal stuff out of the way. I found a lawyer and formed an LLC. I had no idea how to do anything, but I figured it out. I'm really big on making lists: I think that helps me a lot.

AT THE TIME, I WAS RUNNING ON CRAZY ENERGY. I was literally taking the train from my apartment to midtown to the sample rooms a couple times a day, over and over and over again. It was fucking cold, too!

I GUESS I REALLY BELIEVED IN WHAT I HAD TO SAY. I felt like there was something missing, and I didn't like how serious fashion was. I sort of wanted to make fun of it, and be like: "It's not serious, it's just clothes, and I want to make things that make people smile."

THE LEGWORK

ANOTHER ISSUE OF MINE WAS THAT A LOT OF THE BIGGER NAME DESIGNERS AND CREATIVE HEADS WERE MEN. And I was just like, "How do you know what I want to wear as a woman? You can't possibly know." I don't want to wear a really tight shift dress. I would never want to wear that. I don't want to wear the same leather jacket as everyone else. So how do I make it so it's like me?

AS A NEW YORKER, I KNOW WHAT A COAT MEANS. It's a relationship. It's like your boyfriend. You live with it for years. I love coats so much; they're like a second skin. There's also the budget factor. I'm not a big shopper, but when I shop it's going to be for a coat.

I'M FROM NEW YORK: I GREW UP IN QUEENS. But my dad and my grandparents have always worked around the Lower East Side. My dad has a business on Allen and Delancey, and my grandparents live on Rivington Street. I named the Delancey Leather Moto jacket after the street that I sort of grew up on. And then I have all these puffers, I think they're so cool. Grandpas in Chinatown are really big into the puffers, and when I was making this collection I would take all these photos of grandpas.

GROWING UP, MY MOM WAS VERY ANTI-FASHION. She was like, "It's a waste of money, you need to study and focus on good values." She made me feel like it was a bad thing to care about the way you looked, because then you're diverting your attention from what's important.

AS A KID, I SAW FASHION AS THIS UNATTAINABLE THING. And because it was all so unattainable it became that much more precious to me. I think that's what drove me to really fixate on clothes: because I couldn't have those glittery Gap jeans when I was 12!

MY SENSE OF STYLE NOW IS ABOUT PRACTICALITY AND WHAT I THINK IS ELEGANT. When I'm designing my collection it's not like, "Oh, I went to this museum and saw this painting." It's really just whatever I observe around me. It's my neighborhood, it's my friends.

OF COURSE, ANYTHING WORTH DOING IS GOING TO BE STRESSFUL. My mentality is: Take everything one day at a time. At the end of day, you leave your office, you walk around, you go home, and it's not a big deal. It's not so serious, no one's dying. We're making clothing, and my clothes aren't serious to begin with. It's not like this is life or death.

OBVIOUSLY IT'S A BUSINESS, AND I WANT TO BE SUCCESSFUL. I'm extremely competitive to the point where I want to be the best, but at the same time I'm going at my own pace, I'm confident that what I'm communicating to everybody through the clothes is the message that I want to relay. I let the clothes sort of speak for themselves.

I THINK IT'S REALLY IMPORTANT TO HAVE GOOD RELATIONSHIPS. In the short amount of time that I've been doing this, so many people have been so supportive of me, and I'm forever grateful for those people. That makes me want to help out whoever needs my help, too.

WHEN I DON'T WORK, I *DON'T* WORK. I don't want to look at a skirt, I don't want to look at a jacket! I'm just watching TV, hanging out with my dog. Most of my close friends are not in the fashion-related industries at all, and I love that because it makes me feel like a real person.

MY DEFINITION OF SUCCESS IS GOING TO WORK EVERY MORNING AND FEELING HAPPY TO BE THERE. Also, not being bored. One of my biggest fears after graduating college was, "Oh my gosh, am I going to get a job where I just do the same thing every day for the rest of my life until I retire, and I'm bored?" And I'm not. I'm so happy. I mean, I'm fucking stressed out half the time! But I'm still really happy.

WORK IT!

PLAN YOUR WORK.
WORK YOUR PLAN.

By now you've spent some time thinking about what kind of career or big project might work for you, and you're ready to get the ball rolling. So what next?

Turning your ideas into a career takes a lot of strategic planning, and even more hard graft. But there's no reason you can't create a job out of just about anything, so long as you're savvy (and I know you are).

There are a few key steps that will take you from "pipe dream" to "living the dream." They mostly revolve around figuring out how exactly you're going to monetize this big idea of yours, and how (and to whom) you're going to sell your wares once you do.

This is where it's time to get real. Treating your career like a corporation isn't cynical; it's practical, and working your networking is an essential survival skill. This chapter will teach you how to do both.

Every day we're hustlin'.

BE A BUSINESS, WOMAN (EVEN IF YOU'RE NOT A "BUSINESSWOMAN")

Climb Your Own Corporate Ladder

DEFINING THE TERMS OF YOU, INC.

Before we begin to explore how (and why) to approach your career like a business, let's define what a corporation actually is. According to Merriam-Webster's dictionary, it's "a body formed and authorized by law to act as a single person although constituted by one or more persons and legally endowed with various rights and duties including the capacity of succession."

By choosing to pursue a freelance or entrepreneurial path, you are going to have to wear a lot of hats; to act as a "single person" while doing the work of an entire team—even if you do actually have a team.

Going it alone? Congratulations! You're now your own boss, HR manager, marketing officer, and payroll administrator. And if that sounds exhausting, it's because it is. Or, at least, it will be in the beginning. The only way to get your head around juggling all these roles is by treating your career like

a business from the start. Choosing self-employment means going into business as, and with, yourself.

And just as a friendly reminder, the dictionary definition of "business" is: "A commercial or mercantile activity engaged in as a means of livelihood." If you're going to rely on yourself to generate your livelihood, it makes sense to be business-minded from the start.

KNOW YOURSELF, KNOW YOUR WORTH

Thinking about your career as a business will help you to develop a strong awareness of how you think about money, value, and artistry— and, crucially, the relationship between all three.

Essentially, a business plan is a document that outlines how a business is going to achieve its goals. By creating one for your career, you'll be forced to consider tough questions regarding the financial aspects of your setup, as well as your marketing and operational plans.

ESTABLISH YOUR COMPETITIVE ADVANTAGE

You might not like the idea of thinking about your competition at all, but the reality is that the creative industries are rife with talent. In order to build a career with longevity, you need to think about how you'll set yourself apart.

Rather than plotting how you'll outdo the work of others (and thus wind your way into a never-ending downward spiral), think about how you can cultivate your own strengths so that you really shine. What's special and unique about what you have to offer? How can you polish those talents until they sparkle bright enough to capture the attention of your industry or customers?

CONSIDER YOUR STRATEGY

Whether you're just starting up as a freelancer or launching an actual startup, you're going to need a strategy. And in case you're rusty on the dictionary definition of that term, it means: "The art of devising or employing plans or strategems toward a goal."

The use of the word "art" is crucial here: Developing a strategy for your career takes creativity, imagination, and confidence. If you fail to articulate where you're trying to go, you'll work in a perpetual state of self-doubt, indecision, and fear.

Would you try to land a job at a company with no clear structure, business model, or growth plans in place? Probably not. So why embark upon your own creative career without a clear concept of where you might like to end up?

TEST THE MARKET

If you're struggling to commit to your strategy, remember that choosing an approach doesn't mean you have to do the same thing until the end of time; it means you've made a confident, empowered decision to pursue what seems like the best course of action *right now*. Of course, there will be room for adjustment and redirection along the way. The important thing is to have a "master goal" to refer back to in moments of confusion or indecision.

EXERCISE 4:
A Simple Business Plan for You, Inc.

VISION
What are you going to make happen over the course of the next:

ONE YEAR

THREE YEARS

FIVE YEARS

MISSION
Why are you doing this? Whom do you hope to serve?

OBJECTIVES
What are your specific financial and creative goals?
When are you going to achieve them?

WORK IT!

EXERCISE 4: CONTINUED

MARKET
Who will buy your services or products?
Why will they want what you're selling?

USP
What exactly will you sell?
What's your competitive advantage?

LOOK AT ME!
How will you gain the attention of your clients or customers?

EXERCISE 4: CONTINUED

PRACTICALITIES

What are your costs (including materials, labor, and your own living costs)? How do you plan to cover these costs and generate a profit? What will you charge, and how will you grow your profit revenue over time?

PROJECTION$

What are your goals for financial growth?
What do you want to be making in:

ONE YEAR

THREE YEARS

FIVE YEARS

P.O.A.

What's your plan of action? What processes and tasks do you need to engage in to get things off the ground? When and how will you get started?

WORK IT!

PUT YOUR WORK TO WORK
How to Share Your Wares: URL and IRL

Here's some good news: You're already much better at marketing yourself than you realize. In the age of social media, we are all amateur brand-builders—after all, what's an Instagram feed if not an artfully curated campaign for You, Inc.? The trick is turning that "brand" story into one that will get you actual, rent-paying work. Here's how.

STAGE 1→
URL→

POLISH YOUR ONLINE PRESENCE
For freelancers, small business owners, and creative professionals working in the 21st century (i.e., you), a clear, professional online presence is non-negotiable. Devote some energy to really getting this right.

Google yourself (we won't judge you) and view the search results as a potential client might. Is there a link to a public Instagram feed full of drunken party pictures? An old blog you haven't updated in months? A scrappy and incomplete online portfolio? Time to fix it up.

These days, it's so easy to build a slick-looking online portfolio (check the Resources section at the back of this book for sites that can help you), so dedicate at least a couple of days to ensuring your work profile is spick and span. Even if you're in full-time employment, it's worth having a public profile: You never know when you might want or need to pick up freelance work, and you don't want to be faced with building an audience from scratch.

PICTURE YOUR IDEAL BOSS
When you're curating the work that you share online it's important to consider whom you're hoping will see it, and what information you want them to glean. Envision a handful of your dream clients and try to see your site or feed through their eyes. Is it easy to understand what exactly you do? Have you provided enough background

information to take the place of a résumé? Is your body of work cohesive and clearly presented? Would *you* hire *you?* And if not, why not?

RUTHLESSLY CURATE AND EDIT

While it's tempting—especially in the early stages of your career—to share every single project you've ever worked on, you shouldn't. Chances are some of it isn't all that great (ask a blunt friend for a second opinion), and a glut of information can be confusing for an outsider to take in.

Refine your career story to an elevator pitch: If you suddenly found yourself in front of your professional hero with less than a minute to explain what you do, what would you say? This is the story that needs to come across from your online portfolio. Feel free to include personal projects, but ensure that you've incorporated paid commissions as well. Clients need to know that you're able to work within the parameters of a brief while still delivering work that showcases your creative strengths.

CHOOSE YOUR WORDS CAREFULLY

In this hyper-visual era, images are slowly usurping words as the communicative tool of choice. This doesn't mean that words don't

matter. Ensure that your biography, emails, and captions are well-worded and spell-checked. Nothing makes a professional look sloppy faster than an embarrassing typo.

WATCH YOUR FEED

For anyone who isn't a so-called "digital native," chances are that your social media profiles have been a journey of trial and error (we've all looked back at photos and cringed at who might have seen them). But we're now in an age where a messy public profile is a bad look, and people who want you to work for them are absolutely looking at your Instagram account. Keep this in mind every time you upload a public post.

MAKE IT EASY

A potential customer or client should be able to find your contact information in a minute or less. If this isn't the case, fix it immediately. Add your email address to your Instagram biography and a contact form to your website. If people can't reach you easily, they'll just hire someone else.

STAGE 2→ IRL→

GO BACK TO BASICS

Once you've made sure your portfolio is in order, switch your focus to your real-life network. Tell everyone you meet what you're working on (this is called "word-of-mouth" marketing and it's free!). When people know what you're up to, they'll be more likely to think of you when they're seeking someone to do X job/find X service—or if they hear of someone else who might be doing just that.

COLLABORATE

If your portfolio is still looking a bit sparse, build it up with some help from your friends. Collaboration is a great way to share skills and resources, and also stay motivated in the early stages of your career. For example, if you want to make clothes and your best friend is a really talented graphic designer, why not work together to create a print that can be used as the basis for a capsule collection? Or, if you're a writer, work with a photographer friend to produce a 'zine. Projects like these will help you to stay inspired and productive, as well as providing a showcase to the people with the ca$h.

INNOVATE

The days of the traditional résumé are dead. Yeah, I said it. As a self-described creative, use your imagination and skills when it comes to sharing your work. While your online presence is important, a physical product or object is an amazing way to make an impact. Why not collate your best projects,

self-publish a mini coffee table book, and send it to your dream clients? Or make a one-minute video "showreel" of your favorite projects? The possibilities for increasing your visibility are endless. Get inspired, get excited—and watch others do the same.

BUILD AN AUDIENCE

One-off projects are a great way to grab the attention of a dream client, but you'll need to sustain that interest if you want to generate a consistent flow of work. Social media is an obvious way to stay at the forefront of people's minds when it comes to getting hired. Choose a resource that will work best for your own line of work (i.e., Medium.com for writers, or Instagram for graphic designers) and develop a unique way of utilizing that platform for your benefit. Again, be imaginative here: If you're an illustrator, perhaps it's a case of creating a sketch just for Instagram and sharing it on your feed every Friday morning.

Beyond social media, there are lots of ways you can place yourself in your clients' minds. Perhaps you release a monthly newsletter featuring a round-up of all your best projects, or even mail out a beautifully designed round-robin letter at the end of each quarter. The key is to build a consistent calendar of creating and sharing, so that your clients come to expect (and enjoy) your professional updates.

BE YOUR OWN PROOF OF CONCEPT

The quickest way to become a writer/photographer/designer/illustrator? Write. Take photos. Design. Draw.

Perception is reality, as they say. If people can see tangible examples of you doing the thing you want to do, they'll think of you as someone who's already a pro. Of course, high-profile clients and partnerships can provide much-needed legitimacy, but that's no reason why you shouldn't get going on personal projects right now. The truth is that no one is going to give you permission to pursue your dreams, much less push you along the path. Get over your imposter syndrome, and get to work.

THE ART OF PITCHING: FIVE QUICK TIPS

IF YOU'RE GOING TO WORK FOR YOURSELF, YOU NEED TO LEARN TO PITCH.
Whether you're a journalist or a designer, a stylist or a startup founder, at some point you'll have to ask someone to give you money for your awesome project, business, or idea. Money doesn't grow on trees/fall from the sky/land in your lap. You gotta go get it!

The technique you use to ask for this money varies from industry to industry. It might take the form of moodboard PDF, a full pitch deck, or a spoken presentation (and, in some cases, a combination of all three). You'll have to figure out what works best in your field by observing and asking people you respect, but the following five tips apply across the board.

1

DON'T WASTE YOUR TIME ON AN ICE-COLD PITCH

It's OK to approach a brand or business with a totally out-of-the-box idea, but make sure there's at least some form of demand for your concept before you share it. Perhaps you know that an editor is looking for stories, or that a startup is seeking content partners. Maybe you have a great relationship with a company's marketing officer and you know she'd be receptive to your ideas. You don't necessarily need a brief, but you do need a lead.

2

STAY CRYSTAL CLEAR

Creating decks and prepping presentations can be tedious, but it's a very helpful way to ensure that you're super clear on your ideas prior to presenting them. Before you send your PDF or set up a meeting with the CMO, test-run your pitch on a trusted friend. Can he/she grasp your concept in the first minute or less? If not, go back to the drawing board.

3

EVERYONE LOVES A PRETTY PICTURE

A picture is worth a thousand words, as they say. The right imagery will help to set the tone for your concept without you having to litter the presentation page (or your speech) with a glut of textual information. Dedicate time to creating or researching the perfect photos for your concept. The investment will pay off tenfold.

4

PROTECT YA NECK

Ideas get stolen. Sad, but true. Be super careful about showing your big idea to people you don't know and trust—it's very easy to share an email attachment with the rest of the world. Protect your pitch decks by adding a copyright statement in the footer of each slide, as well as your emails. Add passwords and watermarks where applicable. And never submit a full article for consideration!

5

DELIVER ON YOUR PITCH PROMISE

So your pitch went well and you got the job. Congrats! Now make sure you follow through on your original idea (while making room for client tweaks and revisions along the way). If you earn a rep as a person who can conceptualize and execute a totally brilliant creative idea, you'll get hired time and time again.

WORK IT!

EXERCISE 5:
Defining Your Online Presence: Boxes to Tick

PROJECTS Share only the best of the best
Self-initiated projects
Work from only the past three years
Collaborations
Successful client briefs
Projects that showcase the work you *want* to do, not just the stuff you're already doing

PLATFORMS Cover the spectrum and keep it clean
"Clean" Instagram and social media feeds
An up-to-date LinkedIn profile
A simple, curated portfolio site
Contact information that can be found with a Google search in 30 seconds or less

PRESENCE Put yourself in their minds/inboxes
Regularly updated social media feeds—pick your favorite platform and cultivate a strong following
A project that will get people talking
A consistent method for keeping your clients in the loop

WORK YOUR NETWORK
How to Make Connections that Matter

We're more connected than ever before, and yet the act of strategically growing your personal, real-life network still comes with so much stigma attached. "Networking" is whispered like a dirty word, and those who openly seek to build their contacts lists are looked upon with side-eyes.

If you're working for yourself or trying to grow your business, having a strong network is vital to your success. Your ability to make exciting things happen is directly correlated with knowing people who can help you get the job done. When you're grappling with the often stressful reality of executing and monetizing your ideas, a professional network is also a vital source of support. Your mom can't solve all your business-related dilemmas (much as she might try).

That said, there's certainly a protocol that's worth observing if you're actively trying to expand your network. Bear these basic tenets in mind whether you're at a work conference or a birthday party, and you'll watch your contacts list proliferate.

BE INTERESTED

The first tenet on the list is a good rule for life in general. Regardless of what you hope to achieve from a new work-focused relationship, remember that the person you're dealing with is exactly that: a person. Take some time to fill out the full picture by asking non-invasive, personalized questions about your new work friend's life—where did they go to university? What do they think of the speaker you've just heard? What did they have for lunch?—to remind him or her that you're not just some android with a business card.

BE INTERESTING

Then, offer up some compelling information in return. Even the most formal of business arrangements work better when they're established on a foundation of intimacy, and there's no reason why you have to present yourself as if you have no interests beyond work. You don't have to share your blood type and romantic history, but don't be scared to give a little bit of yourself. You'll get a lot back.

"NETWORKING" ISN'T JUST FOR NETWORKING EVENTS

In the same way that apps can make the whole dating experience a little bit less painful (or a whole lot *more* painful, depending on who you match with), targeted networking events can be worth their while. But that's certainly not to say that you should limit your professional outlook to structured events.

Try to go through daily life with an open mind and a goal to learn something from everyone you meet. Don't dismiss people on their appearance or the context in which you meet them—some of the world's wealthiest investors roll around coffee shops in baseball caps and jeans.

BUT! BIDE YOUR TIME

There is a time and a place for talking someone through your business model, and it's not over a cocktail at a mutual friend's birthday drinks. While it can be tempting to try to build a professional relationship with someone you've been desperate to meet for ages when that person suddenly appears right before your eyes, try to be sensitive to the nuances of the

situation. High-profile people are good at sniffing out a sales pitch disguised as a casual conversation, and they'll be forever turned off by someone who crosses that line.

If it feels like an extremely awkward time to approach someone, then chances are it probably is. There are no hard and fast rules, but I'd recommend avoiding the spiel at any event that is definitively personal in nature (weddings, birthdays, funerals); any time after 9 p.m.; and in any environment where people are likely to be uncomfortable and/or preoccupied and probably aren't trying to have *that* talk—doctors' clinics, hectic airports, and so on.

USE THE INTERNET ...

How phenomenally lucky we are to live in an era when pretty much every person you might hope to meet is merely a well-worded email away. The Internet is a fabulous tool for growing your network. Be diligent in using it to this end.

With platforms like Instagram, LinkedIn, Facebook, and Twitter (to list just a few) all offering opportunities to glean the attention of the people we want to reach most, the possibilities for online network-building can be dizzying. But while the World Wide Web might still be a lawless land, you should establish your own boundaries on its use.

Don't "follow up" less than 48 hours after you've sent an email. *Don't* pester people on weekends. *Do* use your creativity to find compelling ways to grab someone's attention (for more ideas on this, see page 56) and to keep it once you have it.

… AND THEN GET OFF THE INTERNET

How many times have you met someone whose online presence was dazzling, confident, and dynamic— only to discover said person was a total letdown in real life? Don't be that person. Don't be a letdown! Strive to make your IRL self a shiny, high-octane version of whatever you put out on the Internet.

How? By not living your entire life through a screen. Go places without taking a photo for Instagram and work on projects without tweeting a link. Build your real life first and foremost, and let your feed offer a mere snapshot of the results. Everyone loves mystery, and you'll be so much more intriguing if you come to the table with interests that you've developed offline.

DON'T CLIMB LADDERS, BUILD BRIDGES …

When you're thinking about how to expand your network, look left and right as often as you look up. Obviously it's beneficial to know people with prestige and experience when you're seeking to

develop your career, but it's also worth remembering that everyone you meet knows something (and someone) you don't.

Look around yourself to find people who seem to have interesting ideas and positive energy, and work with them as much as you can. Building professional relationships with people in the early stages of their careers is a strategic way to go.

… (AND WHATEVER YOU DO, DON'T BURN THEM AS YOU GO)

If you're being proactive about engaging with new people, it's inevitable that you won't get on with everyone you meet. No matter how strongly you feel wronged by someone in a professional context, try to keep your manner cordial at all times.

Obviously you shouldn't let yourself be disrespected, but nor should you react in a way you might come to regret. That person you email in a salty tone regarding a late invoice might end up running the show at an agency you want to be signed by later down the line. Don't let your name leave a bad taste in people's mouths.

BE THE HOST—MAKE THE INTRODUCTION

If you want to meet people, introduce people. Acting as a host

WORK IT!

or connector—whether by inviting a group of women to your house for a dinner party, or putting two friends in touch with a warm email introduction—is a powerful way to see your own network proliferate.

Being generous with your own time, resources, and connections breeds excellent karmic energy. It also tends to reap its own rewards: If you offer up your network as readily as you attempt to tap into the networks of others, people will usually be happy to return the favor.

FIND YOUR CREW

There are lots of associations, member networks, and meetups that you can access online and in real life with a quick Google search. Some are paid, others are totally free, and they might offer anything from physical space to digital resources to private online networks.

Spend some time considering what you need from a network and seeking the one that suits you best. Connecting with likeminded people (especially women) will help you stay motivated and feel supported as you develop your career.

MAINTAIN

Building relationships takes time. Maintaining them, even more so. You don't have to make dinner plans with everyone in your network on a regular basis, but do take the time to check in with the people whose support you value the most. There are myriad ways to do this: with an email, a note in the mail, or even (gasp!) an actual phone call. Send thank-you cards. Reach out to congratulate people on big career successes. Thoughtfulness is always noticed and appreciated.

DEFINE REAL FRIENDSHIP ON YOUR OWN TERMS

As hierarchies crumble and the work/life balance blurs beyond distinction, the realm of friendships can become murky. Where does a work relationship end and a real-life friendship begin? Should you let yourself order a second glass of wine when getting work drinks with a client? Is it appropriate to invite a former employer to your birthday party? Etc. etc. etc.

Again, there's no set protocol for handling these nuances and it's really up to you to draw your own lines. I know people who are connected to seemingly everyone, but can count their friends on one hand. I know others who have 10 best friends and like it that way. However you choose to delineate your social and professional lives, it won't hurt to be courteous and considerate wherever you go.

Madeline Poole

GLOBAL COLOR AMBASSADOR AT SALLY HANSEN

The professional nail artist and creative director on practicing obsessively, teaching herself everything, and the importance of a really strong moodboard

HOMETOWN
Lutherville, MD

CURRENT LOCATION
New York, NY

EDUCATION
BFA in Painting—Maryland Institute College of Art;
Moro Beautify College

EXPERIENCE
• Global Color Ambassador for Sally Hansen
• Author of the book *Nails, Nails, Nails!*
• Designer and creative director

NAIL ART WAS THE FIRST REAL VALIDATION OF SOMETHING I HAD CREATED. I used to paint, draw, and make clothes, and nobody ever thought any of it was cool. Nails were the first time I made something and someone went: "That's cool. I want it, too!" And I was like, "OK, that feels good."

NAILS BECAME AN OUTLET FOR ALL MY DESIGN IDEAS, whether that be color combinations or textures. My mom is a muralist, so I painted a lot of fake turquoise and fake wood growing up, and I've used all that in my work.

MY REFERENCES COME FROM ART HISTORY AND GRAPHIC DESIGN—they're not really beauty references. I do think that sets me apart from other manicurists. I have a whole different slew of inspirations.

WHEN I FIRST STARTED, I HAD NO CHOICE BUT TO DO IT ALL MYSELF. When I did my book there was no budget for a retoucher, so I had to retouch it all myself. And trust me, I didn't know how to retouch.

I PROBABLY AM A CONTROL FREAK. At first I was just really into doing nail art, and felt invigorated by it. But then I started gaining some momentum and realized I needed to stand out and be different from the other people doing this. Part of that is figuring out how to use a computer, use Photoshop, take a good photo.

WHEN IT COMES TO MY APPROACH TO LEARNING, I DEFINITELY TRY TO DO IT ALL ON MY OWN. I don't like to ask anyone. I figure there have got to be directions on the Internet somewhere.

WHEN I FIND SOMETHING I REALLY LIKE, I GET SO DEEPLY OBSESSED WITH IT THAT I CAN'T FALL ASLEEP. From the start of my career I was very, very determined. I became obsessed with learning skills as fast as possible.

I SPEND HOURS JUST PRACTICING. I still sit there on Photoshop all day, just figuring out how to brighten a background, asking myself: "How do I do this correctly?" or watching tutorials. It took years before I could look at a photograph and know if it was colored correctly. If you go back on my website, you'll see that there are photos that are so yellow, or so green. At the time I couldn't see it, but now I've trained my eyes.

I LIKE TO OBSERVE. On photoshoots, I always spy on the photographers and digital techs and try to figure out why they're doing what they're doing. Why are they arranging the lights like that? Why are they using lights and flash?

WORK IT!

I always set out to do something new
and different. There's always a way
to reinvent things, and that should be
a goal for everyone: Be the definitive
version of something, rather than a
reiteration of what's already been done.

OPPORTUNITIES HAVE ARISEN BECAUSE I'M ABLE TO DO A LOT. For example, I think a lot of my paid Instagram gigs happen because brands know I can take a photograph to the standard they require.

I WAS DEFINITELY CONSCIOUS OF CREATING A CONSISTENT VISUAL BRAND. I want everything I do to feel like me. I don't want to be a cheesy nail girl. I wanted to be in charge of all the graphic design, all the imagery, everything on my website.

THERE COMES A POINT WHEN YOU HAVE TO CHOOSE BETWEEN TIME AND MONEY. I really tried to fix my Tumblr so it looked like a professional website, before accepting that it was out of my hands. I just had to wait until I had the money to pay someone to do it.

I'VE DEFINITELY USED MY FRIENDS, BUT I TRY NOT TO ABUSE THEM. I have a lot of friends in all different fields, mostly creative, and they come in handy. It's good to have friends in different places.

THE BOOK-MAKING EXPERIENCE WAS SO DIFFICULT. I was very, very broke at the time. People thought I'd had some kind of success because I'd done famous people's nails, but that doesn't make you any money! It was just at a time when my career was building momentum, but that doesn't mean I was getting paid. I was flat broke, asking for favors left and right. I remember saying: "If you come over and let me do your nails, I'll buy you lunch and do your nails whenever you want." Thankfully, my friends are really easy to please. They're like: "Oooh, lunch. OK."

BY LEARNING HOW TO DO EVERYTHING MYSELF, I'VE DISCOVERED NEW PASSIONS. I love photography—not even necessarily taking the photo, but the entire editing process. I like the design aspect.

I'M A PSYCHO PDF-MAKER. I really love to make moodboards and PDFs in Keynote. I think that has helped me to get a lot of jobs. People love to see that you're so prepared, so if I send over a PDF, everyone's like, "Oh my God, we trust you, do whatever you want." They might ask me to come up with some concepts and bring a piece of paper with a drawing of a fake nail on it, but I'll send a PDF and turn up with a pinboard. People love to see the ideas and concepts, right in front of them.

MOODBOARDING HELPS ME UNDERSTAND WHAT I WANT TO DO, and it also gets me excited. If I'm about to start a huge project, I need one bit of it to be instantly gratifying. A moodboard does that for me.

WORKING WITH A BIG BRAND DOESN'T COMPROMISE MY PERSONAL BRAND AT ALL. It's another outlet. I'm able to keep my style: They hired me *because* of my style. The only annoying thing is I have to keep my hair fixed, because we shoot tutorials all the time. Intense roots do not look good on camera.

I ALWAYS SET OUT TO DO SOMETHING NEW AND DIFFERENT. There's always a way to reinvent things, and that should be a goal for everyone: Be the definitive version of something, rather than a reiteration of what's already been done.

Jen Brill

CREATIVE DIRECTOR, JEN BRILL STUDIO

The hyper-connected downtown creative on setting boundaries, the power of conversation, and the importance of maintaining mystique

HOMETOWN
New York, NY

EDUCATION
Fine Art—Parsons School of Design, NY

CURRENT LOCATION
Brooklyn, NY

EXPERIENCE
• Photo Agent, Total Management
• Artist & Photo Agent at FRED & Associates
• Founder, Jen Brill Studio

WORK IT!

I'M A CREATIVE DIRECTOR BASED IN NEW YORK. I work with brands to create stories—sometimes in the form of a space, sometimes it's a film, sometimes it's advertising. Basically, I have ideas.

I LOVE THE IDEA OF ENERGY IN A VERY LITERAL SENSE. As I've gotten older, I've needed to practice a lot of self-care in order to stay energized. Something I've realized over the years is that I can't run on empty—or if I do, I'll burn out. So on Sunday I have my self-care day. Sometimes I have to force myself, because I do thrive in chaos—it gets me high! But I also know that I need to stop sometimes, and make time for spiritual reflection.

I'VE ALWAYS PUSHED MYSELF TO THE LIMIT, AND ONE DAY I REALIZED IT JUST WASN'T WORKING. It's only recently, in my thirties, that I've started these kinds of practices. I have to force myself to take a holiday in the summer. I have to force myself to take a Christmas holiday. I have to do long weekends. I have to turn my phone off. Those things really work to recharge me.

NO ONE HAS BOUNDARIES IN NEW YORK. If you go out and bump into someone at 10 p.m., they're likely talking to you about business. I actually don't go out very much these days. In the past, if I was at cocktail parties and someone would start to talk to me about work, I'd just use this line: "I don't talk about business after 9:45 p.m."

WHEN YOU'RE A PART OF THE UNIVERSE, THAT'S WHEN THINGS START TO HAPPEN. I always encourage the awesome young women who work for me to leave their desks. Because, guess what? If you sit there telling yourself you need to have an amazing idea, *right now*, it's never going to happen.

I REALLY RESPECT THE IDEA OF MYSTIQUE. It's a cheap trick to tell everyone what you're doing all the time. What's punk, now, is not having a social media presence.

IN LIFE, I'M INTERESTED IN THINGS WITH LOTS OF QUESTION MARKS. Things in people that I can't necessarily define.

LET'S BE REAL: MOST OF THE WORLD IS ATTRACTED TO MEDIOCRITY. If something has a billion likes or followers, chances are that it's not that awesome. Sorry!

I'M VERY PROACTIVE IN MY CAREER. I believe that dialogue and conversation are the keys to success. I'm constantly talking to people, and good things come out of it. And I like to believe that if you produce good work, people will respond to it no matter what.

CONVERSATION IS EVERYTHING. Energy is everything. Have coffee with people. Not because you're trying to get something from them, but just because you want to talk. And all you need is one person to take a chance on you based on something interesting that you've said.

I COLLABORATE WITH PEOPLE ALL THE TIME, AND I DON'T WANT TO SIT AND FLIP THROUGH THEIR BOOK WHEN WE MEET. It doesn't tell me anything. I want to know what you like. Where do you go on vacation? What's the last book you read? What's your favorite song right now? That gives me true insight into someone's character and creativity. A lot of people who work in marketing who would hire someone like me know that. So you talk, and you get to know someone, and you have that creative intimacy. And then you make something awesome together.

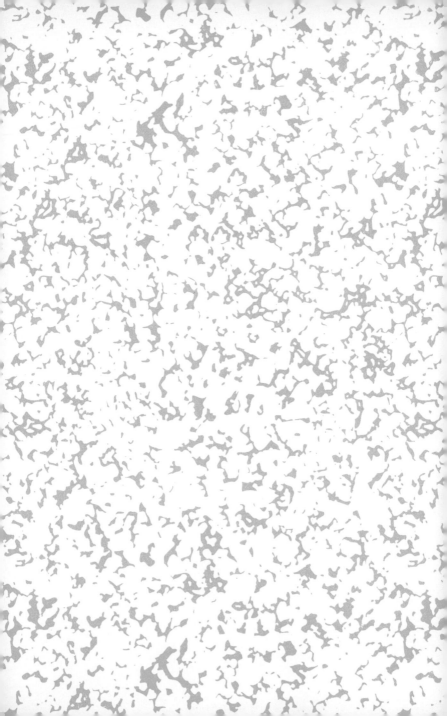

MAKE IT
WORK

MAKE MONEY. SAVE MONEY. SPEND MONEY (AND THEN MAKE SOME MORE).

Whatever your philosophy on life, work, and the transactions that lie between, money is crucial for a happy and healthy existence. Why? Because financial worries are creatively debilitating. Financial instability is massively stressful. And ignorance in this area will land you in a complete and utter mess.

Money doesn't buy happiness, as the cliché goes, but it *does* buy you options. Options are what we want here: options to live where and how we want, to pursue the opportunities that excite us, and (eventually, although this really shouldn't be your expectation in the very beginning) to have total freedom to cherry-pick the work we undertake.

That's why, even if you don't think of yourself as a "money person"—and in fact, *especially* if you don't think of yourself as a "money person"—it's essential to be financially savvy, confident, and informed from the very start of your career. If you're hoping to live off your creative skills in a sustainable and successful manner, you're going to have to get good at getting paid.

Here's how.

RATE YOURSELF
Fix and Finesse Your Rates

WORKING FOR FREE (IN THE VERY BEGINNING)

Unfortunately, the creative industries are rife with unpaid labor and appalling hourly rates. As you cut your teeth, you'll inevitably be asked to work without remuneration. Some people think it's a totally unacceptable practice, and one which undermines everyone working in the creative industries across the board. Others see it as a form of apprenticeship, to be undertaken for a fixed amount of time. It's up to you to decide on your personal philosophy.

If you do decide to create without compensation, *be sure to have clear boundaries about who you'll do it for, and for how long.* Ultimately, it's important to build up a body of non-personal work so that you can sell it later down the line. If you're just starting out, you're probably not producing professional-quality work anyway. So consider taking on a few jobs that will let you practice collaborating with clients and bulk up your portfolio in the meantime.

WORKING FOR FREE (LATER DOWN THE LINE)

Transitioning into your career as a paid creative doesn't mean the end of working for free. In fact, the more successful you become in your chosen field, the more you'll find yourself fielding requests from friends, family members, charities, and even fully functioning businesses, all asking you to work for free, or as good as.

Again, it's up to you to define what a good opportunity really means. Once you've made the transition to paid work, don't look back. If you work for free for one client, another might find out and ask you to do the same. The only person you should be working for without direct compensation is yourself.

SETTING YOUR RATES …

… AKA, the creative's perennial dilemma. Pricing your work is one of the hardest parts of any career. Rates within the creative industries vary wildly from profession to profession, person to person, and place to place. A photographer in New York might be able to command literally 100 times the day rate of a journalist in London, and sometimes even more.

As creative professionals, our work feels personal and therefore becomes even harder to price out. This is where it's helpful to think of yourself as a business (see previous chapter). Not only will this give you an objective sense of the value you can impart and demand, but it will also help you to stay mindful of other crucial factors when it comes to setting your rates.

Imagine you were launching a new brand of coconut water. In order to price each unit, you'd have to consider factors such as your overheads, your production costs, your competitive advantage, and your target market. You'd do research on each of these areas before deciding on your final price.

Apply exactly the same principles when it comes to setting your rates. If you're self-employed, you need to keep a very clear idea of your cost of living in your head at all times (more on this in the next section of this chapter), as well as considering the time and resources you'll have to utilize in order to execute the project, in addition to your relationship with the client. Depending on the nature of the

work, use all these factors to figure out your daily, hourly, or flat rate.

RAISING YOUR RATES

You'd expect to receive a raise every couple of years in a 9-to-5, so why not apply the same principle to your freelance career? No one is going to raise your rates for you, after all. Secure your own Christmas bonus.

If you're working with a new client, the method for doing this is simple: Just ask for a little more than you normally would and see what they say. Don't be frightened of scaring off a prospective client with a higher figure. If he or she truly values your work, the worst they'll do is politely decline and counteroffer.

If you're trying to raise your rates with an existing or regular client, you're going to have to make a case for yourself. Have you invested in a new piece of equipment that increases the quality of your product? Have you learned a new skill that enables you to offer an improved version of what you were doing before? Are you able to work more efficiently? Or, have your own costs of living simply increased? Politely outline whatever your reasoning is, and request adjustments in modest increments. Again, the worst that can happen is you'll receive either a) a counter-offer or b) a no.

HOW TO NEGOTIATE
Dos and Don'ts

Talking about money is hard. You have to learn how to do it anyway. Below are a few guidelines to get you doing it well:

DO remember that everything is negotiable.

DO enquire about your client's budget before you offer up your rate.

DO remember your manners. These people are offering to pay you, after all.

DO outline your worth to the client before the negotiation process begins. Get an outline of what they want, and then explain exactly what you'll deliver.

DO know your worth.

DO stand your ground.

DON'T be scared that you'll lose a job by negotiating the rate. Any employer who isn't willing to discuss money isn't an employer you want to work for.

DON'T shy away from having direct conversations about money with anyone who asks you to work for them.

DON'T be afraid to turn down a job if you feel the money isn't right.

DON'T balk under pressure. This is business, not friendship!

DON'T try to up your salary with your boss or renegotiate your rates with a regular client without good reason (see previous section).

DON'T forget the golden rule: Successful negotiation is about both parties walking away feeling that they got a good deal.

MAKE IT WORK

EXERCISE 6:
An Equation for Calculating Your Hourly Rate

PART 1

(Target annual salary + costs of living & working, including taxes)
/
(Number of total billable hours × 0.75 [figure reduced to allow for
time spent on unpaid work and projects])

PART 2

Adjusted target salary / total billable hours = Target hourly rate

EXAMPLE

PART 1

$75k (£60k) target salary + $3k (£2400) per month living expenses
and $500 (£400) a month taxes × 12 = $117,000 (£93,600)
/
325 days working per year x 8 hours a day = 2,600 × 0.75
= 1,950 billable hours per year

PART 2

$117,000 (£93,600) / 1,950 = Target hourly rate: $60 (£48)
(Or, $480 [£384] target day rate)

(Keep in mind that this rate is based on you being *fully-employed* for
your target number of days spent working per year. For a freelancer,
this number is generally unstable, so adjust the percentage of billable
hours to 0.65 or even 0.5 if this more accurately reflects your average
paid workload—the target hourly rate should go up.)

STACK UP
Ball Within Your Budget. Ball out of Control

CREATING A BUDGET

Creating and living within a budget is an essential aspect of any career. Don't be scared by the idea of this: Knowing exactly how much money you have and where it's going is massively empowering. It's also absolutely imperative to your success—there's no way you'll be able to sustain yourself and your projects if you don't get real about the financial reality of doing so. Like, really real.

Budgets are actually pretty simple to create (see the infographic at the end of this section). Basically, you're just making a spreadsheet that provides an overview of:

A

YOUR NET INCOME

Which means your income after taxes. If you're self-employed, this figure will vary from month to month. There's more guidance on dealing with this below but, for now, use the after-tax figure on your most recent tax return, divided by 12.

B

YOUR FIXED EXPENSES

The costs that you must cover every month, including your rent, utilities, transport, food, etc.

C

YOUR VARIABLE EXPENSES

Money for things that can fluctuate on a monthly basis, such as eating out, entertainment, clothes, and cocktails.

D

YOUR SAVINGS

No matter how broke you are, you should be putting aside a little bit of money into a separate fund each month. Again, more on this below.

Keep this spreadsheet on your computer and download a

budgeting app like Mint (see the Resources section at the back) on your phone to help keep tabs on your spending.

DEALING WITH A VARIABLE INCOME

Perhaps the greatest cause of financial stress for any freelancer or entrepreneur is coping with an income that can vary wildly from month to month. Learning to deal with this is a fundamental part of working for yourself (and the reason so many people choose not to!), but it's up to you to take the reins. Whatever you do, don't try to wing it. Creating a clear and focused method for managing your finances will give you the mental room to do your creative work.

KNOW YOUR BUDGET

Knowledge is power. You need to have an intimate understanding of your own finances and spending habits—to the extent that you could quote your baseline budget off the top of your head if needed. Don't shy away from opening your budgeting app or scrutinizing your bank statement. The anxiety will eat away at you if you refuse to face the situation head on.

SIT ON A CUSHION

If you're planning to embark upon a life of self-employment, you need to start out sitting on a really comfortable financial cushion.

Depending on your prospects, experience, and level of self-confidence, aim to set aside six months' worth of living expenses before you even think about quitting your job.

PRIORITIZE YOUR VARIABLE EXPENSES

Some expenses—your rent, transport, and utilities—won't vary from month to month. But your variable expenses—restaurants, clothes, books, and magazines—should be viewed as negotiable luxuries. Allocate your funds accordingly. It's totally OK to decide that your monthly yoga studio membership is essential, but accept that might mean sacrificing Friday-night happy hour with a friend. Decide what matters to you, and make peace with cutting the rest.

ESTABLISH CONSISTENT INCOME STREAMS

Retainers and regular clients are the freelancer's holy grail. Anything you can do to regulate your monthly income will enable you to make creative and personal decisions from a place of confidence, rather than panic. If you find yourself undertaking similar types of projects for the same people over and over again, then take the initiative and offer your services on a contracted basis. Work hard for people who commission you regularly, and they'll continue to do so. Build trust, over-deliver, and be pleasant to work with at all costs. Most people would much rather employ someone they know than seek a new alternative, even if she comes at a lower day rate.

EMBRACE THE HUSTLE
Presumably, you're choosing a creative career because you prize personal fulfilment and autonomy over the ability to buy a wildly expensive pair of shoes. Yes, you'll probably wake up in the middle of the night freaking out about money sometimes. But you'll also wake up on Monday mornings with the freedom to shape your week into whatever form you please. If that doesn't sound enticing to you, then think carefully before you embark upon this kind of career.

ADDITIONAL EXPENSES: TAX
There are a few things in this life that are absolutely non-negotiable. Paying taxes is one of them. Even if you're earning peanuts, don't be tempted to dodge the taxman. He'll find you eventually!

Employ an accountant to manage your tax return, especially if you're operating a small business. Unless you really love crunching through receipts and spreadsheets, this investment will save you money, time, and stress in the long-term. There's no failsafe way to find a good accountant—start by asking your most financially savvy friend.

Even if you decide to hand over your return to a professional, you must take full responsibility for understanding and complying with the system in your country of residence. You're going to have to deal with tax all your life; ignorance really isn't bliss. Make sure you:

KNOW your entity. Are you filing tax as a sole proprietor (or sole trader in the UK), an LLC/LTD, or a corporation? A good accountant should be able to advise you on the business formation that makes most sense for you, and offer some guidance on how this will impact your final tax return.

DEPOSIT 20-30 percent of every paid invoice into a separate account, just for taxes.

KEEP all your business-related receipts (if you're self-employed, you'll be able to write off a portion of your rent, dining expenses, and travel costs … so essentially, keep the receipts for almost everything).

GIVE yourself plenty of time to find an accountant you trust before tax day. You don't want to rush this process.

ENSURE that you file on time. Late filing penalties can be harsh.

ADDED EXPENSES: DEBTS AND STUDENT LOANS
For many people, debt repayments

MAKE IT WORK

(in the form of student loans or otherwise) can comprise a huge and crippling part of your monthly outgoings. In the US especially, astronomical tuition fees can leave you knee-deep in debt before you've even so much as looked at a credit card application.

BASIC STRATEGIES FOR COPING WITH DEBT

AUTOMATE. Set up a direct debit so that you never have to make a manual loan repayment (*wince*).

DON'T default. Skipping loan repayments will damage your credit score.

ALLOCATE 15–20 percent of your earnings toward paying off debt, if you can. Make the maximum payments you can afford to avoid paying even more interest than you should.

SEEK financial counsel. If you're overwhelmed, get some advice (see the Resources section at the back to find out where).

ADDED EXPENSES: SAVINGS

When you're earning a fluctuating income doing creative work, saving money can seem like a laughable concept. But failing to set aside any of your income—even the smallest amount—means the joke will inevitably be on you. We all get hit

with unexpected expenses, and these can be totally debilitating if you don't have a savings fund set aside to help you cope. Some quick tips for building up your savings, fast:

TIPS

- Factor savings into your budget, just as you would your phone bill.

- Every time you get paid, take 10 percent of the fee for your savings account (plus that 20–30 percent for taxes that we mentioned above. Sorry!).

- Work toward a goal. Saving up for a holiday or major purchase is a good way to incentivize yourself to put money aside regularly.

- Stop buying stuff. It sounds obvious, but you probably fritter money away all the time. Curb impulse spending with the 48-Hour Rule: Anytime you have the urge to buy something that isn't covered by your budget, make yourself wait a full 48 hours before you buy. If you still want it after the time is up (and your budget can take the hit), make the purchase. Nine times out of 10, you'll find you don't really want to!

LONG MONEY

As with building up a juicy savings account, long-term financial planning can seem unfeasible when you have no idea what opportunities might be coming your way in the next three weeks—let alone the next five years.

Just as you should consider your big-picture creative goals, you have to think about your long-term financial ones, too. Do you want to have a child or buy a house? Those things cost money, and lots of it. Don't put too much pressure on yourself by freaking out if you don't have a year's salary put aside, but do take some time to figure out a plan of action for key areas listed below.

FINANCIAL PLANNING

While you may not be able to predict your long-term salary growth and plan accordingly as you would in a "normal job," you can still set yourself clear targets for growing your income as you progress through your creative career.

RAISE YOUR VALUE BY CREATING VALUE

Think about the steps you can take in the next few years that might significantly boost your income in an, "Oh wait, I might actually be able to consider owning property one day" kind of way. This might be anything from raising your annual rates to selling a screenplay

to learning a new, covetable career skill. Try to zoom out and assess where people in your industry generate serious, game-changing wealth. This will vary from profession to profession. If you're a photographer, for example, it might be via landing huge commercial clients. So create a game plan that will set you on that path, even if it might take a long time to get there—we're thinking long money (aka the kind that rappers brag about) here, not handbag money.

RETIREMENT

You're probably never going to be able to retire as a freelancer (kidding/not kidding), but you need to plan for it regardless. If nothing else, money invested in retirement-friendly savings accounts can be written off against your taxes. Would you rather hand over money to the taxman, or your future self? Well, exactly. If you're in full-time employment, be sure to sign up for your company's retirement scheme. If you're not, start putting money into an IRA (US) or stakeholder or self-invested personal pension (UK).

EXERCISE 7:
Build-a-Budget—Basic Ratios for Managing Your Money

YOUR BASIC BUDGET

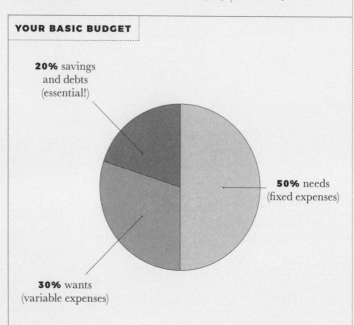

20% savings
and debts
(essential!)

50% needs
(fixed expenses)

30% wants
(variable expenses)

EXAMPLE

After-tax income = **$50,000 (£40,000)/ 12 = $4,166 (£3,333)**

50% needs = **$2,083 (£1,667)**
(no more than 35%, or $1,458 (£1,166), on rent)

30% additional expenses = **$1,249 (£1,000)**

20% savings, debts, investment = **$833 (£667)**

BUILD AN EMPIRE
Self-Employment vs. Startup Life

SO, YOU WANT TO START A BUSINESS

Whether you've already established a successful freelance career or have barely finished school, it's possible that the idea of forming a business has crossed your mind. But do you know what running a business actually means?

If not, it's time to get super clear, so that if you do decide to make the transition you'll be able to launch with the greatest possible chance of success.

FREELANCER VS. ENTREPRENEUR: WHAT'S THE DIFFERENCE?

MAKE IT WORK

FREELANCER

· Get paid for your own work on a project-to-project basis

· Little to no investment required to launch

· Complete one-off tasks and projects, nearly always single-handedly

· Cannot scale output according to demand as the product (i.e., your time and talent!) is finite

· Aim to increase rates and quality of personal commissions over time

ENTREPRENEUR

· Get paid for products and services you've developed and launched in the marketplace

· Investment required to launch (see below)

· Employ and manage a team

· Create a model based on its ability to scale in order to generate additional income

· Aim to create a business that can eventually generate long-term profit and potentially be sold at a later date

EXERCISE 8:
Before You Start Your Business: A Checklist

Now that you have a clear idea of what a business actually means and you've decided you want IN, the real work can begin. This book is about launching and developing a creative career, not a startup, so you'll have to look elsewhere to find all the information you're going to need (see Resources at the back to find out where).

Below is a straightforward checklist that should help you to identify the kinds of things you'll need to think about.

Do plenty of research to ensure your business idea is realistic. If you can't find a comparable product or service because you're "filling a gap in the market," consider why. Is it because there's zero demand? Are the logistics too tricky? Blue-sky thinking is great for creative projects; less so for tenable business plans.

Decide on your model: What are you actually selling, how are you selling it, and at what price? It's amazing how often aspiring entrepreneurs fail to think this part through.

Create a clear and solid business plan that outlines your product or service, marketing strategy, and financial projections.

Test the market. How can you ensure that people want and will pay for your product or service? Figure out a low-cost, low-risk testing strategy and put it to work before you go any further.

Secure investment (see below). If you're bootstrapping, ensure you've set aside sufficient savings to cover all your business overheads and your personal living costs *for at least one year.*

EXERCISE 8: CONTINUED

Choose your entity (LLC, corporation, etc.) and actually form the business. Secure a business tax number. Employ an accountant to do your book-keeping.

File a trademark for your business name.

Line up your suppliers. Whether your product is intellectual, technical, or physical, you'll generate it using information or materials from external sources. What are these sources?

Find a dedicated workspace, even if this just means a corner of your living room.

Consult a lawyer and thoroughly research any licenses, contracts, or clauses you may need to acquire before you start doing business in the country/state in which you operate.

Open a business bank account.

Set up your website, email addresses, social media handles, and any additional tech services your business will require.

You're going to need a lot of support to get this thing off the ground. Assemble a list of people you can call on for emotional or practical help. Is there anyone who can mentor you through the process? ID that person ASAP.

Create a hiring strategy. Even if you can/have to launch alone, you will never be able to scale independently (see the differences between a freelancer and an entrepreneur, page 81). When are you going to take on help, and how?

MAKE IT WORK

BUSINESS INVESTMENT 101
A Jargon-Free Glossary and Guide

TYPE OF INVEST- MENT	WHAT IT MEANS	PROS	CONS	WHERE TO FIND IT
BOOT- STRAPPING	Funding your business using your own finances (credit lines, savings, equity, passive income streams)	No debts to repay Can retain full ownership Quick source of cash flow	Risky (if the business fails, you lose all your money)	In your own wallet
FRIENDS AND FAMILY	Asking friends and family to invest in your business idea, with the debts to be repaid at a prearranged later date	Low/no inter- est rates Fast way to raise small sums	Can cause tension among close friends and family members	In your iPhone's address book
SMALL BUSINESS LOANS	Going to the bank or a loan company to request a lump sum	Good way to secure larger figures without losing owner- ship	Banks are often unwilling to lend to young entrepreneurs If you have to default on your loan repayments, your credit and personal finances will be severely compromised	The bank and/ or businesses that specif- ically cater to you (see Resources)

CROWD-FUNDING	Raising a lump sum through small investments from a large group (usually strangers, via the Internet)	Relatively quick turn-around Can help to generate publicity	If your pledged contribution falls short of the total amount by even a few pounds or dollars, you lose the entire amount You'll usually have to offer a compelling return for your investors in the form of equity or product	Kickstarter, among many others (see Resources)
ANGEL INVEST-MENT	Funding via "angels," aka wealthy business profes-sionals looking to invest larger sums in "the next big thing"—think $10k to a few million dollars	Angels are often willing to invest in "risky" business mod-els that other lenders would pass up Angels are usually entrepreneurs themselves who can offer useful business advice and contacts	Handing over equity with a high expecta-tion of yield	In-person networking and/or angel investor sites (see Resour-ces)
VENTURE CAPITAL	Big bucks investment for businesses seeking $1 million+ to launch; VCs usually invest on behalf of their clients, after hearing a pitch and thoroughly reviewing a business plan in exchange for a compelling ROI (Return on Investment)	If successful, access to large amounts needed to get a global business off the ground	Will require an absolutely watertight business plan VC investors are very, very picky	Seek a referral from a connected business mentor or personal friend

Ann Friedman

FREELANCE JOURNALIST, CO-HOST OF *CALL YOUR GIRLFRIEND* PODCAST, CEO OF LADYSWAGGER, INC.

The journalist and broadcaster on building routines, setting rates, and the concept behind her "Shine Theory"

HOMETOWN
Dubuque, IA

CURRENT LOCATION
Los Angeles, CA

EDUCATION
Bachelor of Journalism—University of Missouri-Columbia

EXPERIENCE
• Executive Editor, *GOOD* magazine
• Deputy Editor, *The American Prospect* magazine
• Editor, Feministing.com

IN MY TWENTIES I WAS DEFINITELY BETTER AT FAKING IT THAN ACTUALLY FEELING CONFIDENT.
I've found a lot of strength in my friends and colleagues. Also, the more risks and chances I take, the better I feel about taking them—even though not all have panned out. The feeling that I'm going to be OK in my career no matter what, even if I suffer a short-term setback, creates confidence.

WHEN I WAS MADE REDUNDANT FROM MY JOB AS A MAGAZINE EDITOR IN 2012, I THOUGHT

GOING FREELANCE WAS A TEMPORARY SOLUTION WHILE I LOOKED FOR ANOTHER FULL-TIME ROLE.
I ended up getting this contract to write a weekly column for *New York Magazine*, and I thought, "Oh, that makes this a little bit more feasible as a real job. Maybe I'll just say yes to this and supplement it with other work and see how it goes." And it went really well!

BECAUSE I'D HAD A 9-TO-5, I KNEW A BUNCH OF CONTACTS ALREADY. It wasn't like I was fresh out of university. Also, I was fired in a pretty high-profile way, so other journalists knew I was unemployed. I think it was a combination of having a network of people who knew me from my days at a staff job, and also that high-profile firing that made people more aware.

WORKING AS AN EDITOR GAVE ME A MUCH STRONGER UNDERSTANDING OF HOW TO PITCH.
In many ways, being a journalist requires the reverse skill set, but I know the mindset of the people I'm pitching to: I know what will keep them happy or make them angry. I know what they're looking for. When I was an editor, I had to think of ideas that were a good fit for the magazine and find the best person to write them. Now, I think of ideas that are a good fit for me and try to find the best place to publish them.

INVEST IN EDITORS AND THEY WILL INVEST IN YOU. I really try to maintain relationships with editors I like, even when they move to new publications or shift their role. Long-term relationships are super valuable because editors like to work with writers they're familiar with. There is always going to be some financial instability with freelancing, but after you've been doing it awhile, you build up a financial cushion so that one late check isn't enough to break you.

I DIDN'T STRUGGLE AS MUCH WITH THE TRANSITION TO WORKING ALONE AS I THOUGHT I WOULD. I spend a lot of time on the phone, either for stories that I'm writing or talking with editors about potential assignments, and sometimes even with other journalists about things that they're writing. And then you're always in touch with people on the Internet.

ROUTINE IS MORE ABOUT FIGURING OUT GENERAL RULES OF THUMB THAN STICKING TO A HARD SCHEDULE. The general rule is that I write better in the morning, but I can make myself do it later in the day if I need to! So I try to schedule interviews and conversations for the afternoon.

WHEN I'M TRYING TO PUSH THROUGH A SLUMP, I'LL SWITCH LOCATIONS. If I've been working from home, I might go out to a coffee shop. For me there's always different types of work to be done. If I'm not being productive writing, I'll say: Maybe it's time to send some invoices or answer emails, or something that's still work, but not the thing I'm doing right now.

I DEFINITELY SUFFER WITH PROCRASTINATION, ALTHOUGH MY WORK AS A REPORTER MAKES THAT HARD. You can't really procrastinate when you have to talk to other people. If I have an article due on Friday then I need to interview people on Tuesday or Wednesday, which means I need to reach out to them on Monday at the latest. Working like that has taught me that you don't have to tackle the entire task in one go—but you should make some move toward the deadline. Once I've taken the first step, I get interested in the subject matter and it's not as hard to write the piece.

I NEVER CONSCIOUSLY SET OUT TO CREATE A "PERSONAL BRAND" AS A JOURNALIST: I JUST SAY YES TO THE ASSIGNMENTS THAT INTEREST ME. I'm genuinely interested in being on Twitter. I wanted to start a podcast with my friend so we could both learn about the medium. I started a weekly newsletter because I thought it would be good to collect everything I had consumed and produced for the week in one place. The common theme is that I'm interested in all these things. There are lots of other things that I'm not that interested in that I don't participate in at all.

SHINE THEORY IS A CONCEPT I ARTICULATED ALONGSIDE MY FRIEND AND PODCAST CO-HOST AMINATOU SOW. She would always say to me, "I don't shine if you don't shine"—meaning she was personally invested in my success and happiness, just as I was in

When I'm negotiating the rate for a new piece, I always ask for more money. Even if what they're offering seems pretty fair. When you're a freelancer, there's no boss who says: "It's time to negotiate your salary for 2017." I negotiate my salary every time I set a rate. Cumulatively it all has to add up to a little more than it did last year if I want to keep growing my income.

hers. Over the years, I've learned that Shine Theory is really a long game. It's been incredible to watch my friends grow in their careers and in their lives, and see how their success also helps me achieve my own goals.

THE SUCCESS OF MY PODCAST, *CALL YOUR GIRLFRIEND*, IS A COMBINATION OF TIMING AND HARD WORK AND LUCK. We definitely weren't the first podcast explicitly to address women, but I do think our combination of tone and topics is pretty unique. We also benefited from the existing networks/platforms that we had. This goes back to Shine Theory—we had a lot of people supporting us and amplifying our work.

MY RULES AROUND SOCIAL MEDIA? I DON'T USE IT IF I'VE HAD MORE THAN TWO DRINKS. And I don't feel obligated to use it every day, or maintain a steady presence. Maybe this works against me, but it's how I stay sane. I have days when I'm on Twitter/Facebook, and days when I just ignore it, or when I read it but don't post anything myself.

WHEN I'M NEGOTIATING THE RATE FOR A NEW PIECE, I ALWAYS ASK FOR MORE MONEY. Even if what they're offering seems pretty fair. When you're a freelancer, there's no boss who says: "It's time to negotiate your salary for 2017." I negotiate my salary every time I set a rate. Cumulatively it all has to add up to a little more than it did last year if I want to keep growing my income.

I LIKE THE IDEA THAT, OVER TIME, MY PER-WORD RATE REALLY INCHES UP. If there's a place I write for regularly but haven't negotiated my rates with for a year or so—while inching up my rates for other places—then I'll just say, "This is way out of step with what I get paid by other places now. Is there any chance that you'd renegotiate?" If you've already got a relationship, it tends to be pretty successful. If they say no, then I'll just write for that place less and write for other places more.

NOW THAT I'VE FIGURED OUT FREELANCING, IT'S HARD TO IMAGINE GOING BACK TO A JOB. I've got a pretty great setup right now, so in some ways the bar keeps going up for how great a full-time job would have to be to pull me away from what I'm doing. But my life could change or my needs could change or my interests could change at any point. I don't think that this is the only work configuration I'll ever have until I retire. If I retire. Actually, retirement is a joke if you're a freelancer.

I'M STILL WORKING THROUGH WHAT IT MEANS TO DO WHAT I DO IN THIS POLITICAL MOMENT. So far, all I've come up with is that it's definitely important for me to keep working, and to use the reporting skills I have to try to answer the questions that are nagging at me. If there's anything I've learned, it's that if I'm struggling with something, other people probably are, too. Which means I should try to examine it in writing.

MAKE IT WORK

Sarah Law

CREATIVE DIRECTOR AND FOUNDER OF KARA

The designer and entrepreneur on the power of follow-up, the importance of common sense, and making handbags for girls who don't own handbags

HOMETOWN
Hong Kong

EDUCATION
BA in Fashion Design—Parsons School of Design, NY

**CURRENT
LOCATION**
New York, NY

EXPERIENCE
• Women's Accessories Designer at Gap
• Founder of KARA

MY BRAND IS CALLED KARA. THE NAME COMES FROM KARAOKE, WHICH MEANS "EMPTY ORCHESTRA" IN JAPANESE. I wanted to use something that was short and memorable, and that makes you laugh a little bit.

I DESIGN HANDBAGS FOR GIRLS THAT DON'T CARRY HANDBAGS. This idea of dying for a pair of shoes and being obsessed with shopping … all that shit I think is pretty weird.

I GREW UP IN HONG KONG AND STUDIED FASHION DESIGN AT PARSONS IN NEW YORK AND PARIS. After I graduated I was runner-up for Parsons' Designer of the Year award. Through that review, I was introduced to Patrick Robinson [then-Head Designer] at Gap and I designed women's accessories there for two and a half years, straight out of college.

I LIKED FASHION, BUT I DIDN'T REALLY HAVE A *SEX AND THE CITY* KIND OF FANTASY ABOUT IT. But I really liked making things, and I always had an interest in a specific look for myself. I remember when I was nine I got really into riding pants and when I was maybe 11, I got really into knee-high Doc Martens. I wore them with everything.

OUR BACKPACK IS REALLY THE LYNCHPIN OF THE WHOLE BRAND. I think it makes sense because it's not a handbag, and it identifies with this girl who is maybe a little bit sportier, a little bit more urban. Sometimes I think of the KARA girl of being like Mathilda from *The Professional*, or Lisa Simpson, or Daria—someone like that. *That* girl totally wears a backpack.

I REMEMBER ALWAYS LIKING THE IDEA OF HAVING A BUSINESS—OF CREATING A WORLD AND MAKING THINGS. But I don't come from a family that was in manufacturing or fashion. Starting my own business was something that I knew I was going to do, but I definitely didn't know all the parts of it.

I QUIT MY JOB AT GAP A WEEK BEFORE I TURNED 25, AND USED MONEY I HAD SAVED OVER A FIVE-YEAR SPAN TO START KARA. At Parsons they really do an amazing job of teaching you how to develop a concept, how to build inspiration, how to sketch the story that you are trying to tell … but they don't talk to you about how to set up an LLC. For a really long time, my cash flow was all saved in this really janky Google doc, and predicting how much things would cost was really a crapshoot.

THE WAY I STARTED THE COMPANY WAS BY BEING 100 PERCENT FOCUSED ON FOLLOW-UP. I would get

I ask a lot of questions. I tell my employees a lot, "'I don't know' is not a wall—it should be a lightbulb in your head." When you say "I don't know," it means you need to ask all these questions in order to move forward. In terms of building a business, I think it's important to look at things that way.

someone's contact information and write them over and over.
The factories that I work with now didn't take me seriously at
first, so I wrote them with updates pretty much every other week
for a year. For sales I did the same thing: I made a list of 300
retailers and for six weeks I literally wrote to every single buyer,
over and over again.

**I WAS DOING OF ALL THIS IN MY APARTMENT, ON
MY BED.** Just continuously emailing, emailing, emailing. Calling.
I think I really developed a very thick skin after that!

**WHAT I LIKE ABOUT BAGS IS THAT THEY HAVE NO
"FIT."** They can be product design, they can be furniture. People
put their magazines in a bag in the living room. There's a lot of
different worlds that bags inhabit that aren't just fashion.

**IT'S REALLY HARD FOR ME TO GO INTO
RETAILERS THAT CREATE CLOTHING THAT JUST
DISINTEGRATES.** You're buying this stuff knowing you're
going to throw it away. Re-using, recycling … I think these are
really important conversations. Seasonality on a weather level—
hot and cold—is real. But seasonality in the sense that "purple is
big, and next year it's green"—that's all bullshit.

**MOST DESIGNERS IN A COMMERCE SPACE WILL
TELL YOU THAT 95 PERCENT OF THE JOB IS NOT
CREATIVITY-BASED.** There was a really long period in the
first two years of running KARA when all I did was focus on
production logistics, like creating an op ex [operating expense],
and human resources, how to hire people, how to fire people,
creating an employee guide, figuring out my benefits. There were
so many foundational things that are still there, and continue to
grow, and need to be looked at, but I've started to realize how
much the company suffers if you don't make design the priority.

**EVERY OTHER WEEK, I HAVE A FULL DAY WHERE
I JUST FOCUS ON DESIGN.** Then throughout every week
there are blocked-out hours when there's absolutely no way you
can interrupt me! I once designed an entire collection in one
afternoon, in my hotel room in China after I'd come back

MAKE IT WORK

from a leather fair. Sometimes the design process has to be focused and concentrated.

THE IDEA THAT YOU WOULD SPEND HUNDREDS OF THOUSANDS OF DOLLARS TO GO TO BUSINESS SCHOOL ... THAT'S CRAZY TO ME. I have a really hard time believing that I could go to business school and they would teach me how to handle the very specific experience I'm having running a business right now.

I ASK A LOT OF QUESTIONS. I tell my employees a lot, "'I don't know' is not a wall—it should be a lightbulb in your head." When you say "I don't know," it means you need to ask all these questions in order to move forward. In terms of building a business, I think it's important to look at things that way.

I DO BELIEVE I CAN ACCOMPLISH THE THINGS THAT I WANT IN MY LIFE. That's a very powerful statement. Now that I have my own line, and I'm doing things in fashion, I believe in it more because it seems real, it's not like an abstract dream anymore. I don't think by any means I've accomplished what I want to in my life, but I believe that I can get what I want.

I'M NOT OBSESSED WITH WORLD DOMINATION. The goal is to run an office, to create a really great livelihood for the people that work within our company, and to become a better designer. To build a real, viable, sustainable business that I live off—that would be my definition of success.

INSIGHTS

Sharmadean Reid MBE

FOUNDER, WAH NAILS

The British businesswoman on confidence, contacts, and learning how to think like a CEO

HOMETOWN
Wolverhampton, UK

CURRENT LOCATION
London, UK

EDUCATION
BA Hons in Fashion Communication and Promotion—University of the Arts London

EXPERIENCE
• Energy Marketing Director at Nike
• Sportswear Editor at *Arena Homme Plus*
• Freelance stylist and creative consultant

I GOT THE IDEA FOR WAH WHEN I WAS AT UNIVERSITY. We had cable TV in our student house, and I remember there were so many hip-hop music videos full of half-naked girls; it was really that era. When my first boyfriend taught me about hip-hop, I naturally gravitated towards the women—the relatively small number of female DJs and MCs. I thought: I really want to document them. Then one day, WAH just came to me: We Ain't Hoes. And I thought, "Yeah, that's sick!" I drew the logo out in bubble writing and it started from there.

I THINK THAT YOUR TWENTIES ARE REALLY ABOUT DISCOVERING AND CREATING, AND CONNECTING AND COLLABORATING. Now I'm in my thirties, I'm quite happy to sit in my office and work, but I wouldn't have been happy doing it in my twenties. I would always have felt as though I missed out on something. I think people right now, they're reading about younger and younger people who are successful, feeling that they need to have that level of success. They just don't.

WHAT I WANT TO SAY TO YOUNG WOMEN IS: DON'T STRESS. I don't want girls to stress about doing things in the wrong order. My life experiences have enabled me to develop the people skills and mental clarity to feel confident that I can run a company of a hundred people in a way that I would never have been able to, had I not gone through that kind of life hardship. It would be easier for me to say that I could have started earlier if I hadn't gone raving—but if I hadn't gone raving, I wouldn't have built up all the people skills and the culture skills to be able to put it in every facet of my business.

I'VE USED WAH AS A WAY TO TEACH MYSELF EVERYTHING. If you're about to start your first business and you have time, you should learn how to do every single thing yourself. I love researching. I get obsessed with things—all I do is read about digital and beauty in periodicals, trade magazines, and weird blogs. I invest money in going to conferences. I just keep my eyes peeled for anything that might relate—including media, art, and music.

I SPEND MOST OF MY TIME READING.
Every time you enter a new industry, it comes with so much of its own lexicon and ways to interact that you really have to learn them. I've done a lot of learning about how the startup world and tech work. I get the game now. Because everything is a game, and you just have to decide if you want to play it or not. If you're willing to do the research, you can do anything.

RUNNING A BRAND AND OPERATING A COMPANY ARE COMPLETELY DIFFERENT THINGS. Before, I didn't really know how to operate a company. I read this book, *What*

If you're worried about people copying your idea, that's the silliest thing. You are a thumbprint. You've seen things other people haven't seen. You've done things, heard things, smelled things, felt things. Whatever you do is going to be unique. I don't ever worry about people copying me. I've got a whole load of ideas. If one of them fails, I can just move on to another one.

They Teach You at Harvard Business School, and I remember thinking: "Should I do an MBA?" Because essentially that's the gap in my knowledge, that type of knowledge—looking at case studies of multinational large corporations and figuring out how they make money and how they structure their companies. Then I was like: I can just read about all the companies that I want to read about, I can just find friends whom I can discuss those things with, and I can just kind of do my own MBA.

I SPENT MY TWENTIES LARGELY BEING A CREATOR, AND NOW I'M DEFINITELY MORE OF A FACILITATOR. You know how people call themselves a boss? I never really felt like I was acting like one before, whereas now I do. I know the level of money I want to make and I know what it takes to get there, and this is what it takes. I want to have money to invest in other companies, I want to have money to be able to buy houses in several countries. I want to have money to be able to do the things and make the things that make me happy. And I know that if I want that type of personal wealth, I need to be running a multi-million-pound company.

TO AMASS THAT KIND OF WEALTH, I THINK THE CONCEPT ALWAYS HAS TO BE TECHNOLOGY-BASED. Product-based businesses are worth a lot of money, but it also takes a lot of work to generate that money. I've shifted from thinking about business-to-consumer to thinking about business-to-business, and I've shifted from thinking about product and service to thinking about software as a service.

I WANT TO BUILD A SOFTWARE COMPANY THAT WILL ENABLE MILLIONS OF PEOPLE TO OPTIMIZE THEIR BEAUTY SERVICES. Software as a service ticks the kind of boxes that please me. It makes me feel good to be able to help other people's businesses. It suits me to work in my office on a grand plan, and then release it to the world.

WITH SOFTWARE, WE COULD RELEASE FEATURES EVERY SINGLE DAY. I like that because I like to move fast and I'm very addicted to newness. If someone keeps talking about the same shit to me, I lose interest very quickly.

WHAT MAKES ME FEEL POWERFUL? Well, right now what's bolstering my confidence is that I know I do good shit, even if everyone doesn't see it.

I'VE ALWAYS ENTERED MALE-DOMINATED WORLDS. I've played football my whole life, I've always done things that boys have done. I also like being a big fish in a small pond, and I think that when you enter a male-dominated world, the pond of women is usually small. Then you can create your own environment within that industry, and I really want to build a company that does as well as any male-led company.

IN MY OPINION, GETTING SOMETHING DONE IS JUST AS RESPECTABLE AS DOING SOMETHING WELL. I see magazines all the time that are shit, but do you know how hard it is to make a magazine? I just think: "Well done you." Done is better than perfect. What value is an idea that exists in your head, where no one else can see it?

I DON'T BELIEVE IN FAILURE. I hate it when people talk about that. I think you decide if you want to do something or not. If something's not working out for you, and you don't want to do it anymore, then fine, end it.

I TELL ABSOLUTELY EVERYONE WHAT I'M DOING. I never hide things. I've got so many friends who are like, "Oh yeah, I'm working on a big project that I can't tell you about." And I just think, "Well, that's crap. Because I'm not going to see you for six months, and in that time people are going to ask me what you're up to, and I won't have anything to tell them." So there's no word-of-mouth marketing, which is crucial.

IF YOU'RE WORRIED ABOUT PEOPLE COPYING YOUR IDEA, THAT'S THE SILLIEST THING. You are a thumbprint. You've seen things other people haven't seen. You've done things, heard things, smelled things, felt things. Whatever you do is going to be unique. I don't ever worry about people copying me. I've got a whole load of ideas. If one of them fails, I can just move on to another one.

WORK
WELL

LEARN. IMPROVE. EVOLVE.

Ours is an age of instant gratification. We're obsessed with the new, the trending, and the 'Gram-able—whether that means the hot It Girl photographer, or the latest superfood craze.

Unfortunately, our love of the refresh button has led to a decreased willingness to stick out the boring bits and tolerate the necessary grind. If genius is in fact 1 percent inspiration and 99 percent perspiration, how can we find the inspiration we need to actually *do the work?* And, just as crucially, to get better as we go?

Maintaining and evolving a successful creative career is just as hard as launching one right off the bat. Once you've shared news of your exciting new project on Twitter, you've got to crunch your way through the daily process of making it happen—and hopefully enjoying the ride along the way.

So, how can you get inspired and stay inspired? Improve the quality of your work every day? And find the courage to start again when you're burnt out or just plain bored? This section has some ideas.

WATCH YOUR INTAKE
Nourish Your Creative Mind

EAT YOUR (CREATIVE) VEGETABLES

Trash in, trash out. Just as you wouldn't eat cheeseburgers for dinner every night and expect to wake up with glowing skin, you really can't expect your creative mind to function on a high level if you're constantly feeding it with junk. We all like the odd reality TV binge and endless scroll, but don't let this make up the majority of your cultural intake. Aim to consume a "rainbow plate" of inspirations as nutritious as a spread of organic vegetables.

Consume books, photography, good films, and music. Go to museums, galleries, talks, and shows. Read books by authors you love—and then books by the authors that they love. Commit to looking after your creativity just as you would your physical health, and you'll see results in the quality of your ideas.

And just as you'd give yourself rest days from your workout regime, be sure to take regular breaks from taking in new information, even when it's of a really high caliber. Sometimes, it's good to just lie around and zone out.

GIVE YOURSELF VISUAL CUES

It's relatively easy to find inspiration when you open your eyes and mind to it. The tricky part is infusing that sense of motivation into your daily life, so that it can do its job of galvanizing your creative work.

Make the process simple by placing visual cues everywhere. Whether this means inspirational words on Post-It notes or a moodboard above your desk is up to you. Just ensure your inspirations are in your frequent eyeline so that you don't have to go hunting for new ones each day (and likely fall down an Instagram rabbit hole).

KNOW YOUR REFERENCES

If you want to do better work, create with a sense of context and concept. Even if you're working with new technology and contemporary cultural ideas, there's always a precedent to be explored and learnt from.

While you're hatching plans to launch your big idea, take a moment to look backward as well. How have other people manifested similar concepts using different formats? Who is considered the master of your art form? What historical or technological shift gave birth to the tradition in which you now work?

Thinking about this stuff will enrich the quality of your work. Even if your references aren't obvious on the surface (and they shouldn't be, unless in an act of explicit homage), you'll be all the more creatively confident by just knowing that they're there.

TAKE BREAKS

A lesson you don't want to learn the hard way: Burnout is a real thing. No matter how busy you are, you must factor in time to rest your mind.

How much rest you take, and the way you take it, is up to you. Just don't delude yourself into thinking that you don't need any at all. Don't feel pressurized into working around the clock by stories of tireless entrepreneurs that you read about in magazines. Yes, you might have "as many hours in the day as Beyoncé"—but you definitely don't have the same number of staff.

Know your body and your own limitations. If you feel demotivated when attempting to tackle your workload and the feeling lasts longer than a couple of days, in all likelihood you need a break. Take a full day off at least once a week, and try to factor in a longer breather every two to three months, especially if you run your own business.

TRAVEL AND EXPLORE

If you're struggling to find inspiration in your immediate surroundings, chances are that you need to get away from them. Travel is one of the fastest ways to replenish your creativity, and you don't have to spend three weeks exploring Southeast Asia to reap its benefits. Short, well-timed breaks are a highly effective way to replenish your juices and get your ideas flowing again.

If you're working for yourself the notion of "time off" can seem laughable, but try to remember that you're just as deserving of vacation time as your salaried friend. Just because you're "following your dreams" doesn't mean you don't get to take a break from them. The pressure of marketing your creativity can be immense; seeing a new part of the world won't solve your problems, but it will throw them into relief.

EXERCISE 9:
A List of Inspirations: Things / People / Places / Spaces

Keep your list of inspirations within easy reach. When you're feeling down or depressed, just take a glance at it and do/meet/visit/see one thing on it.

THINGS (Books / Artworks / Songs / Photographs)

1 _____   2 _____

3 _____   4 _____

PEOPLE (Family / Friends / Colleagues / Mentors)

1 _____   2 _____

3 _____   4 _____

PLACES (Cities / Parks / Beaches / Homes)

1 _____   2 _____

3 _____   4 _____

SPACES (Galleries / Museums / Libraries / Institutions)

1 _____   2 _____

3 _____   4 _____

WORK WELL

UP THE ANTE
Doin' It, and Doin' It, and Doin' It Well

HOW TO GET REALLY GOOD AT YOUR WORK

Quite simply? Keep working.

You're not going to be very good at whatever it is you do right when you start doing it, so let go of any notion that you should be. It doesn't matter if your articles, photos, artwork, or illustrations aren't as good as you'd like them to be in the beginning: What matters is that you keep creating.

You're probably familiar with the 10,000-Hour Rule, which states that approximately 10,000 hours of practice are required to become world-class in any field. Put into context, that means practicing for eight *solid* hours a day, *five days a week*, over a span of *almost five years*.

Whether you subscribe to this theory or not, remember that mastering any craft takes years of dedicated study and devotion. If you're not willing to spend a long time practicing your craft with little reward or acknowledgment—and

to make the necessary sacrifices for your bank balance or social life along the way—then you should rethink your big career plan.

BE A SUCCESSFUL MULTI-HUSTLER

There's no argument over the fact that focusing on one thing is a much faster way of getting really good at something than trying to do a lot of different things at once. But if you do want to do a lot of things at once, don't feel the need to limit yourself. Just be smart about the way you balance your time.

We now have self-publishing tools that enable us to create, share, and sell our work in any medium we wish—an incredible gift for a creative person. And nowadays, many career paths require multi-skilled workers who are equally confident editing a batch of images *and* writing the captions to run alongside them. If you're launching your own business, you're going to have to learn how to wear all the hats. All at once. All the time.

So, how to embrace the multi-hustle without losing your mind?

BREAK IT DOWN
First thing's first: Get crystal clear on what you're doing, and what still needs to be done. For each of your current projects take a blank sheet of paper, open a blank document, or start a new Note in your app of choice and list every single task between now and completion. There! You probably feel more organized already.

PICK YOUR TOOLS
Some people like to project manage with multiple notebooks. Others like whiteboards. Some keep it all digital. Whatever your favorite organizational tool, it's worth consolidating all your thoughts into one place so you can keep track of stuff on any given day (or device).

TIME BLOCK
There are lots of ways to approach project management, but the only one that almost certainly won't work is endlessly jumping from task to task, never really finishing or making much progress on any, and exhausting your brain in the process. Depending on the consistency of your to-do list, it might be worth blocking out certain days to deal with certain types of work, for example Mondays for Project A, Wednesdays for Project B. Obviously this schedule can be adjusted according to deadline, but giving yourself a full day to tackle a project is generally more productive than spending 20 minutes on this and 20 minutes on that, ad infinitum.

GO ON AUTOPILOT
When you're making endless creative and administrative decisions on a daily basis, your brain can become easily fatigued. Combat this by automating as much of your daily schedule as you possibly can: your breakfast, your workout, your working hours, etc. When you don't have to map out every single moment of your day anew each morning, you'll have more mental energy to deal with the stuff that matters.

REMEMBER WHY YOU STARTED
There's no doubt that juggling lots of different projects can be stressful, but it's also highly stimulating. Whenever you're freaked out about having "too much" going on, try to remember the alternative: not having *enough* going on. Stress is preferable to mental sedation any day of the week. Pick your poison! Then make your plan.

BECOMING AN AUTODIDACT
With technology transforming industries faster than people can break into them and higher education becoming unaffordable for all but the moneyed elite,

contemporary working culture requires us all to become autodidacts. Fortunately, it has never been easier to access the information you need to develop your skills, further your career, and become a really interesting dinner-party guest in the process.

Autodidacticism—i.e., self-directed learning—is not an easy pursuit. Teaching yourself anything requires a huge amount of dedication and discernment. But it's an essential requirement for a creative career … and it can also be really fun.

Don't overload yourself by trying to absorb too much information at once—one topic at a time is more than enough to tackle. You might choose something that directly relates to your career path (if you're writing a novel, perhaps you want to read the full works of your favorite writer) or something you want to learn more about, just for fun.

Try to spend three months reading, watching, and digesting all that you can on that subject before moving on to the next topic, which might well be an offshoot of whatever movement/period/school of thought you've just explored. Or perhaps it'll be something totally new. Following your curiosity and your imagination wherever they take you is crucial to staying enthused and engaged.

FINDING A MENTOR

We all dream of finding someone who might gently guide us throughout every stage of our creative careers, offering great advice and a wise sounding-board along the way. Unfortunately, such figures are pretty hard to come by. People are busy, and work is changing fast. Even our most respected elders might not seem like the best candidates to advise us on excelling in career paths that didn't even exist five years ago.

But don't feel alone! There are ways of finding the guidance you seek. The first is simply to look left and right at your peers (and maybe even backward, to the younger generation coming up behind you). Chances are that you have people in your immediate professional and personal circles who are really good at what they do. Start with those people.

A little secret: Everyone loves being asked for advice, especially if it seems tailored specifically to their own areas of expertise. So don't be afraid to ask your successful accountant friend how to tackle your taxes, or your younger cousin with the crazy Instagram following for her top social media tips. They'll be flattered and eager to help.

When it comes to establishing more traditional mentorships, seek to build a strong relationship with someone you already know and with whom you've begun to develop a mentor/mentee dynamic (a good rule of thumb for finding a mentor is that you should never have to actually *ask* someone to be your mentor—the relationship should develop organically).

Try to schedule regular meetings with someone who has shown an interest in your work, or previously championed you in some way. Ask them thoughtful questions about areas that are troubling you, and then (and this is crucial) *implement their advice*. No one likes to waste their time counseling someone through a situation, be it a silly career move or a bad breakup, only to see their thoughts and words deliberately ignored. To find a good mentor, be a good mentee, both in theory and in practice. Take advice graciously, apply it efficiently, and generally aim to offer a good return on investment.

If there's no one in your life that you feel you can turn to for help, there are also lots of organizations and platforms that provide business and career advice to young people trying to get their start in the creative industries (for more information, check out the Resources section at the back).

PLAY THE LONG GAME
How and When to Keep Going
(vs. Knowing When to Stop)

DON'T BE A CAREER COMMITMENT-PHOBE

It's so exciting to start something from scratch. A new project feels light and pure, full of potential to become the best thing you've ever done. But life can't all be launches, fresh starts, and clean slates. In order to get really good at something and grow it to its fullest potential, you're going to have to learn how to play the long game.

In your twenties especially, life can feel way too unpredictable to make long-term plans. You probably don't even know where you'll be living next year, let alone what you want to have achieved in the next decade. But don't let your lack of vision excuse a total lack of commitment. By all means try new things (jobs, cities, lovers, friends), but also avoid skittering about too much when the going gets tough. You can create a strategy without having total clarity on your ultimate aim. You just need to ensure you're always moving along a thoughtful, self-aware path (and making regular pit stops to

evaluate your progress along the way).

No matter where you're at in your career, you probably have a strong idea of your key interests and skills. Find an intersection between those two elements, and start building on it. Don't worry about a super-defined end goal; focus on a theme instead. This might be as broad as "community" or as specific as "botanicals." Do as much as you can to build a niche for yourself in the context of this consistent thread.

Set goals and stick with them until they reach fruition—doing so will bolster your personal confidence levels. Stay true to your values and your passions (see the first chapter) and you'll be surprised by the amount of cohesion you'll see when you look back.

PLATEAUS AND BURNOUTS

These are an inevitable phase in any project or career. You *will* get incredibly bored of what you're doing, and the thought of tackling your workload every day *will* reduce you to tears. This happens to everyone. If you're currently going through either phase, one of two things could be happening:

> **1**
>
> You're no longer sufficiently challenged.
>
> ....
>
> **2**
>
> You're totally exhausted and/ or overwhelmed.

It's crucial to identify the difference before you ditch whatever you're doing and start again. Persistence is what distinguishes a successful person from a not-so-successful person. Before you walk away, make sure that you're not just abandoning the path you're on because it seems too difficult. It's part of your job to decide what's working and what's worth working on, or else you risk regretting having given up too soon in a year's time.

It's up to you to draw the line between "tough patch" and "total disaster," but ask yourself a few key questions before you do:

- Does your work have a positive impact on the lives of others?
- Are you able to financially support yourself through what you do?

- Is there room for creative and financial development in your chosen career path?
- Does your job align with your personal values?
- Have you recently hit a pothole you hadn't anticipated, but one that can feasibly be resolved with a bit of elbow grease and grit?
- Does your job support the lifestyle you want to lead (or can it be tweaked in order to do so)?

If the answer to most of these questions is "yes," then there's a lot of leverage left in what you're doing and you're probably just wiped out. Schedule some real time off ASAP (heading off on holiday with your laptop in tow doesn't count) and spend at least a week resting your mind, eyes, and soul. If you return to your desk *still* feeling dispirited, it might be time to think again.

STARTING OVER

Maybe you've spent some time evaluating your options and decided that you're really and truly ready for change. You might be 10 years into your career, or six months into a really big project—either way, making a decision like this takes bravery, so props to you.

Wherever you're at, remember the famous expression: "It's never too late to be what you might have been." With the exception of a couple of very niche professions (prima ballerina; Hollywood child star) there's nothing to stop you from pursuing any line of creative work at any point in your life.

The only mistake you can really make is repeating your past mistakes and expecting different results; everything else is just a lesson. So before you jump into a new profession, ask yourself what's behind the change of heart. If you want financial stability and your previous career wasn't providing it, what will make the new line of work any different? If you're over feeling totally stressed out and overworked, why are you even contemplating starting a new business?

Everyone is capable of—and entitled to—a fresh start, so by all means make one if you wish. Just ensure that you're taking the time to lay down solid new foundations rather than just wallpapering over the cracks.

MEASURING (AND MARKING) SUCCESS

What does success mean to you? This is one of life's biggest questions.

The answer will change many times throughout the course of your career. You'll second-guess yourself. You may well achieve something that once felt like a lifelong dream, only to be left feeling curiously numb. Creative people tend to have incredibly high standards, rendering us unable to feel "successful" with any sense of ease. If you're your own boss, the gauge is even more difficult to measure. With no one to give you a positive career review or tell you you're doing well, how can you possibly know if you are (or, more worryingly, *aren't*)?

For better or worse, we're living in a time when success is increasingly gauged in social media metrics. Followers and "likes" have become the barometer of popularity and relevance, especially in the creative sphere. This is a precarious value system—subscribe to it at your peril.

If you want to live a contented creative life, stay focused on your own path. Stop comparing yourself to others. Develop a thick skin. And try to remember—every day—that pursuing a life of creativity is a privilege and a pleasure. Live and work with joy.

INSIGHTS

Penny Martin

EDITOR IN CHIEF OF *THE GENTLEWOMAN*

The illustrious EIC on developing peculiarities, building a wide knowledge base, and the merits of a life lived backwards

HOMETOWN
Born in Glasgow and raised in St Andrews, Scotland

CURRENT LOCATION
London, UK

EDUCATION
MA (Hons) in History of Art—Glasgow University
Postgraduate Diploma in Art Gallery & Museum Studies—
 Manchester University

EXPERIENCE
• Editor in Chief, SHOWstudio.com
• Curator, The Fawcett Library
• Curator, The National Museum of Photography,
 Film & Television

I'VE LIVED MY LIFE BACKWARDS, REALLY. I started earnestly as an academic, working in the dark towards this idea of the greater good—working on a project or a piece of work, sending that off to central filing, and knowing it might not be seen for 60 years until that file was opened back up. I certainly didn't have any expectation of publicity or personal profile.

THE WAY THAT I APPROACHED MY CAREER WAS TOWARD EXCELLENCE AND EXPERTISE—AND BLOODY HELL, I WORKED. I was at university on and off

Develop a particular kind of peculiarity, otherwise nobody will think of you as the obvious choice for anything.

for nine years and I worked on my hands and knees, in the dark, in archives for what felt like forever.

I WAS DOING A PHD AND IT HAPPENED THAT I HAD A STROKE OF LUCK AND WAS ASKED TO WORK FOR NICK KNIGHT AT SHOWSTUDIO [the fashion film website where Martin was Editor in Chief from 2001–08]. I walked away from that intensity and insidiousness of academia into lightness, pace, and fun. I'm really lucky. I would never have known that would suit me.

I THINK THERE COMES A TIME WHEN SPEED AND REACTIVENESS AND SPONTANEITY STOP BEING PARTICULARLY NOURISHING IN THE LONG TERM. SHOWstudio was great for a time in my life, but I originally came from museums and was really interested in returning to a longer project.

WHEN THE ROLE AS EDITOR OF *THE GENTLEWOMAN* CAME UP, THE INTELLECTUAL SNOB IN ME RESPONDED TO THE OPPORTUNITY OF WORKING WITH [PUBLISHERS] JOP VAN BENNEKOM AND GERT JONKERS. They are brilliant journalists, they are unrelenting taskmasters, and they are never happy with anything they produce.

THE FIRST THING THAT GETS DISCUSSED AS SOON AS THE MAGAZINE COMES IN THE DOOR IS WHAT COULD HAVE BEEN BETTER. It's such an un-triumphant, un-celebrity culture, despite being a happy, fun, and joyful place. People perceive the fashion industry as being rather pleased with itself and champagne o'clock in the late afternoon. *The Gentlewoman* is the opposite.

THERE'S NOT REALLY A UNIFYING CHARACTERISTIC OF THE WOMEN WE PROFILE; THAT COMES FROM THE DESIGN CONTEXT AND THE PHOTOGRAPHY. What makes our Beyoncé cover have any relationship whatsoever with our Angela Lansbury one is candid imagery, a non-sexualized approach to styling, and humor.

IT'S A KIND OF COMMUNICATION THAT ISN'T A PROVOCATION TO BE LOOKED AT. There's intelligence in [our cover stars'] eyes, and they understand what that cover means. These women are not being looked at in spite of themselves; they're completely part of that exchange. I hope that's clear.

WHERE DO OUR STANDARDS COME FROM? I think it's partly about not wanting to repeat ourselves, and partly about being inspired by what you hate! You can see when people are using their publication very explicitly as a shop window for all their consultancy; that's really cynical and depressing. It's about making sure you never find yourself doing that.

I WAS ALWAYS EXPECTED TO HAVE KNOWLEDGE ABOUT THE ART WORLD AND THE DESIGN WORLD. I think those are the qualities that separate me out from other journalists who are far better writers than I am. I have a wide knowledge base as a result of having aspired to just be good, rather than rushing after my career and spending all my ideas down the rabbit hole.

IF ALL YOU KNOW ABOUT IS HOW TO MAKE A MAGAZINE, THERE'S NOTHING UNUSUAL ABOUT YOU. Develop a particular kind of peculiarity, otherwise nobody will think of you as the obvious choice for anything.

I WORRY ABOUT YOUNG PEOPLE RUSHING INTO CAREER-BASED DEGREES THAT ONLY GIVE YOU THE CHANCE TO BE WORKERS, RATHER THAN THINKERS. Treat your education as a route to a job because you'll need it for other things—especially your second job and your third job, when you really have to turn to your thinking skills.

I SUPPOSE THE MORAL OF THE STORY IS THAT YOU NEED TO LEARN YOUR TRADE BEFORE YOU HAVE ANY EXPECTATION OF IT PAYING OFF. That's a very difficult piece of advice to be giving a generation of people who didn't get a free education like I did and will be paying enormous university fees. But learning to have that knowledge base is really what will see you all the way through your career.

INSIGHTS

Piera Gelardi

**EXECUTIVE CREATIVE DIRECTOR AND
CO-FOUNDER, REFINERY29**

The digital media maven on coping with
overwhelm, self-care rituals, and why we should
all be celebrating our successes

HOMETOWN
Biddeford, ME

EDUCATION
Bachelor of Science in Studio Art—New York University

**CURRENT
LOCATION**
New York, NY

EXPERIENCE
• Photo Director of *CITY* magazine

**PEOPLE OFTEN ASK: DID WE KNOW IF REFINERY29
WAS GOING TO BECOME WHAT IT BECAME, AND
DID WE HAVE SOME BIG PLAN?** The answer is that it's a
two-part thing. I feel like someone who's putting one foot in front
of the other in one sense, but I'm also very ambitious, motivated,
and intuitive. As much as I don't know what the future looks like,
I know that if I closed my eyes I'd still get there.

**THE GROWTH OF THE BUSINESS CAN BE OVER-
WHELMING.** What's interesting is that as you start to see your

dream happen and your career develop, the vision for it gets bigger and bigger. Once that vision starts to crystallize it can be really difficult to know how to make that into a reality, but I think that is ultimately about prioritization.

I THINK ABOUT THE BIG GOALS, THE BIG THINGS WE'RE TRYING TO ACCOMPLISH OVER, SAY, THE NEXT TWO YEARS. THEN I ASK MYSELF: WHAT ARE THE PIECES OF THAT PUZZLE? Week to week, I look at the big pieces that will lead up to the two-year goal. And then I commit to certain things that will connect to the two-year vision. Things will always come up and derail you to a certain extent, but if you break it down you can figure out what can be moved around, and what needs to stay put.

THE WORLD IS CHANGING VERY RAPIDLY. On a bi-weekly basis there's news that shifts the way that industries work. I always think about the fact that my great-grandfather was a carriage-maker in Italy, a very successful one, and then the automobile became a thing and all of a sudden he had no business. My family moved from Italy to the US and became fruit-sellers. That happens all the time. It's important to have a vision for what you want to do, but also to be really aware of what is changing in your industry and in the world so you can continue to adapt.

A COUPLE OF YEARS BACK, WE HAD OUR 10-YEAR ANNIVERSARY. A PR person actually warned us against publicizing how old we are because there are a lot of media companies that are popping off, right off the bat. I do think that 10 years is not very long when you compare us to amazing brands. There's so much knowledge that's been gained through the time that we've been building our business.

I THINK THERE'S AN UNDERSTANDING NOW THAT YOU HAVE TO BE SKILLED IN A LOT OF AREAS IN ORDER TO BE SUCCESSFUL. It's not just your skills in graphic design that are going to propel you in your chosen career, but also your skills in leadership, your presentation skills, your business skills. There's a perception that you can achieve instant

I feel like someone who's putting one foot in front of the other in one sense, but I'm also very ambitious, motivated, and intuitive. As much as I don't know what the future looks like, I know that if I closed my eyes I'd still get there.

success now, but a lot of times that kind of success is transitory. For people who do want to develop their careers over the long term, it's still about developing your craft along with a broader suite of skills.

I GREW UP IN AN ENTREPRENEURIAL FAMILY.
When I was younger I would hang out in my dad's factory, so work and life were always meshed together. For me, having them mixed up works.

CELEBRATING YOUR WINS IS SO IMPORTANT.
Sometimes when you have a big dream you can get so caught up in it, like: "I'm not there yet, I don't know all the things I want to know, I haven't hit all the goals I want to achieve." A big part of endurance is about marking those milestones. In life, it's important to celebrate those milestones and figure out how you want to reward yourself.

FOR ME, SELF-CARE IS ABOUT RITUALS. Every morning, I make coffee and fried eggs and I listen to a podcast as I'm getting ready. It's just a little bit of time, but giving that to myself in the morning puts me in a much better place than when I used to jump out of bed, run and grab Starbucks and be drinking coffee and eating a weird doughnut at my desk.

SO OFTEN, WE CAN FOCUS ON WHAT WE'RE NOT GOOD AT AND WHERE WE FEEL WE'RE LACKING, WHEN WE SHOULD BE FOCUSING ON OUR SUCCESSES. When you have a great day where you feel really productive and amazing, what were the factors that helped you to accomplish that? It's all about trying to replicate those for yourself, playing to your strengths, and knowing the things that make you function at your best.

INSIGHTS

Kai Avent-deLeon

FOUNDER, SINCERELY, TOMMY

The store owner and designer on seeking stimulation, celebrating sensuality, and staying in her own headspace

HOMETOWN
Brooklyn, NY

**CURRENT
LOCATION**
Brooklyn, NY

EDUCATION
Fashion Design—Fashion Institute of Technology, NY

EXPERIENCE
• Sales Assistant at Addy & Ferro
• Operations at Aritzia
• Retail Operations at Chanel

SINCERELY, TOMMY IS A LIFESTYLE CONCEPT STORE. We're home to amazing, emerging designers—whether that be clothing, jewelry, or home goods—as well as artwork from around the world. We also have a coffee counter inside, so it's really a communal space. We want people to just come and hang out and explore everything that we have collected and whatever we are doing. We really encourage that sense of community.

I'M ALWAYS LOOKING TO BE STIMULATED. Someone told me once that that could be my downfall! So when I'm looking at art or spaces, I'm just seeking to see something very different. I like looking at ways of doing something differently, whether it's how an architect I love lets light into his home, or very abstract artwork. Anything that makes you dig a little deeper.

THE STORE IS ALWAYS CHANGING. I think when it first opened it was a little more playful. Now it's not serious, but it just has a maturity. I think that's because I'm growing personally. I'm embracing being a woman and loving that, and I'm really inspired by all the women around me and the stories that they tell me from their lives.

WITH THAT EXPLORATION, I'M ALSO EXPLORING MY SEXUALITY AND WHAT THAT MEANS TO ME. The clothing I sell now is much more about being comfortable and playful in how you wear clothes. There is a lot of linen and silk. You know you see these beautiful Italian or French women with these very loose silk dresses on, and a strap kind of fallen down? That moment when a woman can really feel sexy and comfortable with who she is? That's where the store is, because that's where I am.

I DESIGN OUR IN-HOUSE LABEL, WHICH IS ALSO CALLED SINCERELY, TOMMY. When it started we were offering really cool basics, but now I'm more concerned about the textures and materials that we're using, because I'm also concerned about a woman feeling good in what she's wearing, and feeling really confident.

I NEVER STARTED THIS BECAUSE I THOUGHT, "OH I'M GOING TO BE A BOSS, I'M GOING TO BE A BUSINESSWOMAN." I did it because I was passionate about clothing and art and beautiful things, and that was my main priority for opening this store. And I've had to learn to be a businesswoman along the way.

I FEEL LIKE THE MORE YOU PUSH FOR INSPIRATION, THE LESS YOU'LL FIND IT. I try not to put too much pressure on myself. If I'm feeling stuck maybe I'll go to yoga, maybe I'll watch films. Those are always a stimulant for me.

I GREW UP IN BEDFORD-STUYVESANT, BROOKLYN, WHICH IS ALSO WHERE MY STORE IS. I was a weirdo growing up, big time. Every activity that I expressed some interest in, my parents put me in a class for. My dad is also a huge film buff, so he was showing me Woody Allen and Pedro Almodóvar and all of these really great directors from a very early age. I think that helped develop my taste.

I BUY THINGS THAT I LOVE RATHER THAN BUYING THINGS TO MATCH. IF I LOVE IT, THERE'S A STORY THERE, AND IT WILL ALWAYS WORK IN THE SPACE BECAUSE I'M CONNECTED TO IT. I've also reduced the amount of things that I buy. When I was younger it was more about the name or the cost, and now it's much more just finding things that I really love, and knowing that they're going to be with me for a long time.

AT THIS POINT I REALLY JUST WANT TO BE ABLE TO TRAVEL AND NOT FEEL TIED DOWN TO ANYTHING. Staying light and having the flexibility to move when you want to is my definition of freedom right now. I'm trying to make sense of that in relation to the store, because it's my baby. But also I'm a floater and a free spirit, so I'm trying to figure out what that looks like as a business owner.

I THINK I'VE ALWAYS BEEN GOOD AT STAYING IN MY OWN HEADSPACE. Maybe to a fault actually … I kind of just do what I want. I'm coming to understand that I'm always going to have to be in a situation, whether it's family or work, where I can travel, and just kind of do my own thing when I want to. Because I need that freedom—to be able to do Kai time.

Sandeep Salter

FOUNDER & DIRECTOR, PICTURE ROOM

The store owner and consultant on time management, tempered ambition, and the true meaning of elegance

HOMETOWN
London, UK

CURRENT LOCATION
New York, NY

EDUCATION
BFA in Fine Art—Parsons School of Design, NY
BA in Philosophy—Eugene Lang College of Liberal Arts at
    The New School for Social Research
MA in Creative Publishing, Criticism and Journalism

EXPERIENCE
• Part-time professor, The New School
• Art, Design, and Architecture Buyer at McNally
  Jackson Books
• Bibliographer at Printed Matter

I CO-FOUNDED TWO SHOPS: Goods for the Study, which is a stationery store: everything for your home, office, workspace. Picture Room is a shop for artwork and editions, objects, anything that falls under the category of things made by artists. I founded the stores with Sarah McNally—she's also the owner of the bookstore McNally Jackson around the corner—but now I run Picture Room independently.

I STARTED WORKING AT PRINTED MATTER WHEN I WAS A SENIOR IN COLLEGE. It's the oldest shop and nonprofit for artists' books in New York, and an institution for printed works by artists. It's one of the most incredible resources for anybody who is coming in interested in book-related work, or publishing practices.

FROM PRINTED MATTER, I WENT STRAIGHT TO WORKING AT MCNALLY JACKSON AS THE ART, ARCHITECTURE, AND DESIGN BUYER. Also, during that time, while I was at Printed Matter I set up Cambridge Books near MIT [in Massachusetts], which was a bookshop for art theory. That was my first retail endeavor of my own.

AFTER THAT I WAS AT MCNALLY JACKSON, DOING BUYING FOR AROUND TWO YEARS BEFORE WE OPENED GOODS FOR THE STUDY. Sarah and I just work so well together, we're good friends and we've always collaborated really smoothly. We don't have exactly the same taste, but we have a very, very similar aesthetic.

WHAT I WOULD HOPE ONE WOULD FEEL WHEN THEY'RE IN EITHER OF THE SHOPS IS A SENSE OF WARMTH. And somewhere comfortable. But there's nothing craftsy there. Craftsy is not a word I would like to be associated with!

WHAT'S A WORD I WOULD LIKE TO BE ASSOCIATED WITH? ELEGANT. I THINK THAT "ELEGANT" IS A VERY SPECIFIC WORD. It has its own academic history and architectural history because it should be something that is functional and beautiful. That's a word that I find very useful when informing my buying. It's efficient.

WHEN WE WERE FIRST BUYING FOR THE STORE, THE UNDERLYING THING THAT SARAH AND I WOULD ALWAYS COME BACK TO WAS: "DO WE LOVE IT?" And if we loved something then it would pass the test. But if we felt even an ounce of indifference towards something, then no. I still feel like that has been the most useful tool. Both of us are incredibly intuitive about all of what we do; we've never made a business plan.

Often people who are ambitious
can be impatient and work very hard
to get somewhere. That's one way
of doing it, and I certainly work super
hard, but in a tempered way. I don't
like to let things get to me.
I've never lost a night's sleep.

I DON'T REALLY STRESS OUT TOO MUCH ABOUT WORK. There's a lot at stake—and then there isn't. When I put it into perspective I think, "We're just so lucky to be here on Mulberry Street, with the shops of my dreams, and they're actually working." Beyond that I don't really think there's much to sweat.

OFTEN PEOPLE WHO ARE AMBITIOUS CAN BE IMPATIENT AND WORK VERY HARD TO GET SOMEWHERE. That's one way of doing it, and I certainly work super hard, but in a tempered way. I don't like to let things get to me. I've never lost a night's sleep. Even in school, never.

I THINK TIME MANAGEMENT IS A BIG PART OF STAYING CALM. I work really fast and hard when I'm here. I set little goals like taking lunch—that's something that has carried on since I was a little kid. I'll tell myself, "This is a block of time that you have; you don't have time to go eat right now. So if that's the goal, then you wait and eat at the end of the day." It really helps me to just knock things out.

I THINK THAT MAYBE OUR GENERATION HAS A LOT OF EXPECTATIONS OF THINGS BEING ENJOYABLE ALL THE TIME, AND I DON'T [laughs]. I've had relationships in the past where people have been unwilling to just get on with it and do the work, and I have never had that problem. I would just work.

MY ADVICE FOR ANYONE HOPING TO OFFER A CURATED RETAIL SPACE WOULD BE TO TRY TO BE VERY CLEAR ABOUT WHAT YOU WANT IN THE SPACE. Be specific, have an idea, and go for that idea. And don't be afraid to tell people that their ideas don't fit into your idea.

WORK WELL

WORKING ON 100

BALANCE YOUR HUSTLE AND YOUR HEALTH

Best health is best practice. This is one of the New Rules of Work listed at the front of this book, and it's probably the most fundamental of them all. Building a successful, self-made career means looking after the wellbeing of the business, especially if "the business" = you.

"Best health" means something different for everyone. Figuring out the "best practices" for achieving your own state of optimal wellbeing will be a journey of trial, error, and constant tweaks. Don't feel guilty about taking the time to do this work. It's an invaluable investment.

As your career evolves and your body changes, your techniques for maintaining optimal wellbeing will probably have to be adjusted, too. The only real way to make sure you're always feeling and working on 100 is to have constant check-ins with yourself. There's an endless pool of "wellness" information out there, but try not to treat it as gospel truth. Nobody knows your body better than you.

That said, there are some basic rules and established principles that will help you to build a strategy for feeling positive, strong, and inspired on a daily basis. Cherry-pick any of the ideas included here that you like the sound of, and mix them up with your own personal rituals and routines.

TODAY WAS A GOOD DAY
Have a Productive Day, Every Day

WHY ROUTINES MATTER

Even if you're not used to having "office hours," trying to establish an independent working routine can lead to indecision bordering on existential crisis. Creating your working life from scratch is a conundrum with endless variables, after all. How many hours should you be putting in? Are weekends sacred, or for the weak? What should you work on when you don't have any paid projects underway? And so on, and so on, and so on …

The level of routine you'll require to combat this type of angst is entirely up to you. Even if you're confident in your ability to get things done without too many self-imposed rules and regulations in place, it's good to establish some non-negotiable rituals from the start. As the expression goes, "Any decision is better than no decision at all." That way, when your workload amps up unexpectedly or life throws a stressful situation your way, you'll have a personal "employee's handbook" to refer to.

A solid routine is also essential for achieving your goals. Without a clear sense of what you're going to make happen in any given month or week, you'll lose your days in a flurry of reactive busywork: answering emails, posting on social media, and taking meetings with no end goal in sight.

For nearly all of us, a structured life is a productive life. There are countless romantic notions tied to the creative lifestyle: global travel, chic coworking spaces, writing to-do lists in far-flung locations. But, mostly, creative success is like any other type of success—a matter of sitting down in one place, day after day, and *doing the work*.

GOAL-SETTING GUIDELINES

Setting goals alone can be daunting. This basic structure should help (and, for more assistance, see the first chapter).

VISUALIZE ANNUALLY (OR BIANNUALLY)

Once a year, sit down to plan your

big goals. These are the major things that you hope to achieve over the course of the next 12 months. Think big, but be realistic. Trying to open a boutique, write a novel, and a buy a house in the space of one year is a fast track to a stressful life. For optimum success and the greatest chances of happiness, choose one professional goal (something career-related), one personal goal (something related to home life, love life, health, or friendships), and one habitual goal (something you want to do—or drop—on a daily basis).

PLAN QUARTERLY

You probably already know that businesses typically use "quarters" to break up the financial year. These three-month chunks are abbreviated to Q1, Q2, Q3, and Q4, with earnings and dividends reported at the end of each one. Whether you're running a business or not, quarters are a really helpful way to plot your progress throughout the calendar year. Three months is enough time to make real progress, but not so long that you'll lose track of your "big picture" goals along the way.

It also makes sense to align your goals with the season. While some tasks (email, admin, bookkeeping) must be completed whatever the weather, others are best suited to certain times of year. There's not

much point in trying to launch a womenswear brand in August when the entire fashion industry is on holiday, for example. Trying to get people to kick into action just before Christmas can be impossible, while September is a great time of year to offer educational tools and services to coincide with the "back to school" kick … you get the gist.

When you set quarterly goals, it's worth adhering to the basic principles of S.M.A.R.T. planning. This means checking that everything you write on your list is:

SPECIFIC

✖ Finish book.

✔ Complete research and write text for chapters 9 and 10 of novel. Allocate two weeks to edit all copy.

MEASURABLE

✖ Relaunch portfolio site.

✔ Email friends to find a web designer by end of January. Work with the designer throughout February. Launch new site by end of March.

ASSIGNABLE

✖ Improve social media presence.

✔ Personally create a moodboard providing an overview of the desired social media presence. Commission a freelance social media assistant to be responsible for all assets.

. . . .

REALISTIC

✘ Buy a house.

✔ Revise budget to allocate a higher proportion of earnings into a savings account for a deposit.

. . . .

TIME-RELATED

✘ Work out regularly.

✔ Commit to four yoga classes every week for the next three months.

a folder on your hard drive, where you're sure to forget all about them.

CREATE ACCOUNTABILITY
This is especially important if you're working alone. Within reason, create check-in points throughout the week to keep your routine on track. Meet a work buddy in a coffee shop every Friday morning. Pre-pay for an exercise class. Hire an assistant to help you every Wednesday. In general, make a commitment to yourself and your routine. You'll feel so much stronger for having done so.

REVIEW WEEKLY
There's no worse feeling than waking up on a Monday morning in a state of abject panic about the working week ahead. Take 20 minutes every Sunday to review your quarterly plans and block out specific tasks under certain days. Make sure you take any prescheduled meetings and personal commitments into account when you're allocating your tasks for each day (for more on planning a great week, see Exercise 10).

INCREASE VISIBILITY
Now, put your goals somewhere you can see them. This might be on a Stickies note on your laptop desktop, or on a whiteboard in the corner of your workspace. Just make sure they're not hidden in a file in

EXERCISE 10:
A Week that Works

Basic principles for planning an effective week:

- Incorporate a non-work-related morning routine dedicated to your personal wellbeing. This could take no more than 20 minutes. Do it every day.

- Identify "peak energy" periods and dedicate them solely to creative work.

- Create boundaries around when you'll take meetings. Don't schedule them for peak energy times.

- Create accountability via a standing work date with a freelance friend.

- Block in exercise and book classes in advance so you don't get tempted to skip them.

- Give yourself at least one full day off a week.

So your weekly schedule might look something like this ...

	FIRST THING	A.M.	P.M.	EVENING	DAILY
MON	Gym	Undisturbed creative work	Pitching / email follow-ups	Cook at home / prep for week	Drink a liter of water first thing Meditate for 10 minutes, twice a day
TUE	Walk to work	*Peak energy* Hardest task of the week	Hardest task of the week, cont'd	Dinner with friends	Don't check social media before 12 p.m.
WED	Yoga at home	*Peak energy* Hardest task of the week	Work admin (ordering supplies, sorting finances)	Yoga	Read something that's not on a screen Get outside for at least 30 minutes
THUR	Reading	Undisturbed creative work	4 p.m. meeting	FREE	Eat one meal mindfully
FRI	Gym	Work party with free-lance friend	(Every other week) Creative strategy and research	FREE	List three good things about the day before you go to bed
SAT	Yoga	FREE	FREE	FREE	
SUN	Make plan for week ahead	Life admin (laundry, shopping, personal care)	FREE	FREE	

TIME MANAGEMENT
Essential Principles

1
LIVE IN THE PRESENT

If you fail to stay present, you will be forever stuck in a time-scarcity trap. Your attention will be lost in a quagmire of future-focused fear, while your daily to-dos will escape your attention. Practice meditation and incorporate regular mindfulness breaks into your daily routine to avoid this common pitfall.

....

2
TIME BLOCK

When planning your weekly schedule, lump together similar tasks in order to avoid too much mental branch-swinging. Jumping from pitching to social media to meetings will run you into the ground. Instead, block out certain days for focusing on specific areas of your career (i.e., Mondays for pitching and proposals, Tuesdays for digital projects, Wednesdays for creative work, etc.).

3
GET UP EARLIER

The simplest, most effective way to squeeze more out of your day? Get up earlier! When you read up on the daily schedules of successful people, there's a reason you'll find that nearly all of them get out of bed by 7 a.m. or earlier: It's a no-nonsense hack for getting stuff done. Not a morning person? Train yourself by making your alarm time earlier in increments of 10 minutes each day, and avoiding extra long lie-ins on weekends.

....

4
SCHEDULE SELF-CARE

Allocate fixed time in your schedule for exercise, preparing healthy food, or doing whatever else it is you need to do to feel sane. These practices are as crucial to your ongoing career success as any others.

5
CHOOSE YOUR ENVIRONMENT

Get familiar with the types of work you do best in certain environments. Perhaps you like writing in bed or stretched out on the sofa, but prefer to be at a desk for planning and emails. You might be able to create moodboards in a noisy coffee shop, but find that focused creative work requires absolute calm. If you don't have an office or other fixed workspace, try to build your weekly routine around the places and spaces that work best for you.

....

6
IDENTIFY TIME DRAINS

If you constantly get to the end of the day feeling as if you haven't even begun to get through your to-do list, take a hard look at where you're losing time and address the drains. Are you spending too long getting ready to leave the house? Figure out a 30-minute morning routine. Are you wasting hours commuting? Consider working from home. Wherever time can be saved, save it. On which note …

....

7
GET YOUR SOCIAL MEDIA INTAKE UNDER CONTROL

Chances are, you're spending a lot of time on your phone—probably more than you're comfortable or happy with. Create some rules around your phone usage to find a more comfortable balance. This might be as simple as avoiding Instagram and Twitter before 12 p.m. Set your emails to "fetch," not "push" to your phone. Leave your phone in your bag rather than on your desk. Go for walks without it. The world will not crumble around you.

....

8
OUTSOURCE AND DELEGATE

Effective delegation is crucial to long-term success. Whether you're running a team of 20 or one, there are certain tasks that are worth allocating. If nothing else, making yourself delegate will force you to be really clear on what needs to get done (and to keep your control-freak tendencies in check). Whether it's getting your groceries delivered or hiring a social media assistant, take a look at where you can pass the buck.

....

9
SWITCH OFF

Build a hard "stop" time into your schedule, and try to observe it each day. Knowing that you're going to be turning off your laptop at 7 p.m., whatever the weather, will provide the incentive you need to power through your working day.

10
CUT STUFF OUT

One way to have more time is simply to cut stuff out. Women are particularly prone to the pressure to have and do it all: to thrive in our careers, have "perfect" bodies, maintain active social lives, and be flawless partners, mothers, and homeowners. Needless to say, it's impossible to achieve this level of perfection without making yourself miserable. Make peace with not being able to do everything, and then cut one thing out of your schedule (anything that doesn't bring you happiness and/or decent money is a good place to start).

....

11
GET CLEAR. STAY COMMITTED

By all means dedicate time to creating concise plans (see the next section for more details). But once you've made your plans, stop fiddling with them. Stop adding stuff. Don't let a competitor's latest Instagram post make you reevaluate your entire plan for the year. Set your goals, and get on with them.

....

12
LET GO SOMETIMES

There will be times full of looming deadlines, and last-minute opportunities will make the idea of a regular schedule seem laughable.

Learn to accept this fact. Know that there will be days, even weeks, when you'll have to order in food and skip the gym. But once you've crunched through whatever extenuating circumstances have caused you to cast aside your personal routine, make sure you find your way back to it, and quickly. In the opposite direction, burnout awaits.

LOOKING AFTER #1
How to Feel Amazing: 20 Easy Tips

1
Get enough sleep.

2
Find a form of exercise you like and do it most days.

3
Don't drink too much alcohol or coffee.

4
Spend time with people who uplift you.

5
Spend time alone doing things that make you happy.

6
Find a form of meditation that works for you and practice daily.

7
Breathe.

8
Leave your phone at home sometimes.

9
Meet friends in real life (don't just text).

10
Say no to things you don't want to do.

11
Take proper breaks.

12
Drink water. Lots of it.

13
Share meals with people whose company you enjoy.

14
Declutter your home and workspace regularly.

15
Every time you feel the urge to complain, vocalize a solution to the problem instead. If there's no solution, don't complain.

16
Spend time in nature.

17
Stimulate your mind with high-quality books, TV, films, and art.

18
Celebrate your successes (and life in general).

19
Help other people.

20
Say thanks.

SELF-CARE STRATEGIES FOR SUCCESS

PRESENCE > PRODUCTIVITY: USE SELF-AWARENESS AS THE ULTIMATE CAREER TOOL

There's a vast amount of information on nutrition and wellness out there, so this section is by no means exhaustive. Every body is different, and the needs of women's bodies in particular are constantly evolving. The foods, exercises, and rituals that make you feel amazing at 21 might stop working for you at 41.

For this reason, the most important thing you can do for your body is to develop a keen awareness of it. The goal is to feel as "in" your body as possible, so that you make fewer decisions that take you away from a state of ease and optimal comfort in your skin. The best way to get to this state is through mindfulness about your daily choices (see below) and regular self-reflection. On days when you feel particularly great or especially not-great, consider:

? What is occupying your thoughts? Are there any serious concerns or issues that are affecting your ability to think clearly?

? Whom have you engaged with, and what impact did the interaction have on your state of mind?

? What did you eat for your last three meals? How did you feel when you were finished?

? Did you sleep well last night? And the night before?

? If you're feeling stressed, what email, call, person, or situation triggered that emotion? Where in your body are you feeling the stress?

? When was the last time you exercised?

? How much time have you spent looking at a screen in the past 24 hours?

? When did you feel best in the past week? Where were you? What were you doing? Whom were you doing it with? How can you repeat those circumstances again in the near future?

By staging regular check-ins with yourself, you'll be able to identify what makes you feel your best (and your worst). Once you've recognized positive patterns, you can build your working life and personal routine around them.

MINDFULNESS AND MEDITATION

You've likely read enough about the endless benefits of meditation, so they won't be espoused here. Needless to say, it's one of the most beneficial habits you could possibly acquire. Incorporating it into your daily routine is a very cheap, constructive way to improve concentration, reduce anxiety, and generally increase your sense of joy and pleasure in everyday working life.

Start with just 10 minutes a day. Sit quietly and focus on your breath as it rises and falls. When your focus lapses (and it will), catch yourself as your mind begins to wander. Go back to your breath once again. Repeat. Practice again tomorrow.

IT'S ALL IN YOUR HEAD: TIPS FOR MAINTAINING OPTIMAL MENTAL HEALTH

Working for yourself can cause an immense amount of stress. Not only are you coping with a fluctuating income and schedule, you're also in charge of making endless decisions, day in and day out. On good days,

this level of autonomy can seem like the ultimate freedom. On bad days, you'll feel as if you're heading for a nervous breakdown. Given the high-pressure stakes of a self-made creative career, take extra care with your own mental health.

Many of the practices and routines listed in this chapter will help you to feel happy and functional, but it's also worth remembering to:

– LEAVE THE HOUSE
  When you work from home, it's tempting to sit down at your desk first thing and stay there until your eyes start to blur. Try to get some fresh air and a new perspective at least once a day. Go out for lunch. Walk around the block. Spend 30 minutes in your nearest park.

– CREATE YOUR OWN RITUALS
  The lack of structure that comes with self-employment can be exhausting. Create your own steadfast rituals to bring a sense of rhythm and consistency in your working day.

– CHECK IN WITH OTHERS
  Schedule a bi-monthly brainstorming session with a friend. Plan a weekly work party around your kitchen table or at a nearby cafe.

- OBEY YOUR ENERGY
  LEVELS
  One of the best things about
  setting your own schedule is
  being able to work at the times
  that suit you best. Don't force
  yourself to stick to a 10-to-6
  day just because you've been
  institutionalized to do so. If
  you're an early bird, start at
  8 a.m. and clock off at 4 p.m.
  If you know you can't think
  straight until at least midday,
  do all your creative work from
  then on. If you love working on
  Sundays when everyone else is
  chilling out, work then and give
  yourself Mondays off.

- BE A GOOD BOSS TO
  YOURSELF
  You wouldn't expect an employee
  to work 14-hour days and skip
  meals entirely, so why push
  yourself through the same thing?
  Treat yourself with kindness
  wherever possible. You'll be far
  more effective as a result.

- TACKLE SELF-DOUBT
  AND LOW SELF-ESTEEM
  HEAD ON
  Self-employment will force you
  to get to know yourself really
  well, really fast. If you find
  yourself consistently getting
  anxious about the same tasks or
  procrastinating on a daily basis,
  explore what's at the root of this
  fear and self-doubt—then get

to work on breaking down these
thoughts through consistent,
positive action and affirmations.

MANAGING SOCIAL MEDIA AND TECHNOLOGY-RELATED ANXIETY

Many of us have a conflicted relationship with technology. We all spend far too long staring at screens. At the same time, few people would dispute the fact that smartphones and apps have made our lives more convenient and connected than ever. Regardless of where you sit on the spectrum, it's important to incorporate regular "digital detox" breaks to ensure that you don't become a slave to the refresh button.

RETHINKING YOUR RELATIONSHIP WITH TECHNOLOGY: A FEW QUESTIONS TO ASK YOURSELF

? Which of your technology habits most frequently creates anxiety for you? Is it the amount of time you spend online, or the things you're looking at? (Likely it's both, but try to pinpoint the source of discomfort as accurately as you can.)

? Think back over the past week. Was there a particularly negative feeling you experienced directly in relation to something you saw or read online that particularly altered your mood? Trace the steps of that experience. How can you minimize repeat scenarios in the future?

? How is social media beneficial and pleasurable for you? How can you continue to enjoy these benefits, without falling prey to the aspects you listed above?

? How do you need to use social media for your career? Are there ways you can organize yourself so that you can do this more efficiently and effectively? Or perhaps outsource it entirely?

? When was a time you regretted oversharing some aspect of your personal life online? What led you to do that? How can you avoid doing it again?

? How much time (honestly!) do you spend looking at your phone each day? Are you comfortable with that number? If not, how can you reduce it?

? Which "offline" activity brings you most satisfaction? How can you incorporate more of it into your daily life?

SOCIAL MEDIA 101
A Basic Protocol

Attend to the basics: turn off notifications.
Change email from "push" to "pull."
....

Close your Gmail tab while you're working.
Check email at three pre-defined times a day.
....

Leave your phone in your bag when:
· At the office.
· With company.
· Eating meals.
· In the bathroom.
· In the bedroom.
....

No, but really: no phone in bed. Charge it outside of
your room. Buy an alarm clock.
....

Create a social media schedule for your work.
Try not to divert from this.
....

Once a week, leave the house without your phone.
Go and get a coffee for an hour. The world won't end.
....

Creation before consumption. Don't read any emails, news stories, or text messages until you've created one thing for yourself each morning. Even if it's just your breakfast.

....

Call sometimes. Text less.

....

Don't use your phone when you're waiting or in short-haul transit, and avoid the temptation to do so, e.g., before you leave your house for a commute, put on a podcast and then tuck your phone away in your bag, out of hand's reach.

....

Replace a negative habit with a positive goal. Instead of thinking: "I won't look at my phone after 8 p.m.," dedicate your evenings to reading, watching movies, or cooking. Staying mindful of the time you regain for pleasure will galvanize you to reduce the time spent online.

....

Stop comparing: followers, number of posts, general volume of content. This is applicable to both business and life. Yes, social media is an essential career tool. No, you don't have to adopt the aggressive "sharing" protocol you've read about on some random marketing website. Don't want to post four times a day? Don't post four times a day. Simple.

....

Don't take it all so seriously.

....

WORK/LIFE
The Art and Myth of Balance

ON "HAVING IT ALL"

Work/life balance: What does it even mean? The simple answer is: Whatever you want it to mean. Whatever you *decide* it should mean. It's likely—because circumstances change and people do, too—this meaning will shift and evolve many times throughout your working life.

Choosing to pursue a creative, self-made career means taking full responsibility for your own time, and the value you ascribe to it. It's up to you to define how many hours of the week you allocate for "work" and how many you file under "life." Some people need a strong division between the two in order to be happy and productive. Others prefer to work intensely for long stretches, forgoing any real personal life, and then do absolutely nothing for days on end. Very few people flourish without some sense of structure in place, but you get to decide for yourself.

As with all elements of an autonomous working life,

figuring out the best balance will probably be an ongoing process of experimentation. Sometimes you'll get it right for a few weeks or months: to-do lists will get ticked off, you'll get eight hours' sleep a night, and you'll make it to the gym four times a week. Then, something might come along and totally upend that balance: a family emergency, a big commission—or, on the opposite end of the spectrum, a quiet spell that might last months on end. You'll have to recalibrate quickly to your new reality, neglecting one area of your life while you attend to more pressing concerns in another.

Whatever your definition of work/life balance looks like, you'll need to be comfortable with blurred boundaries. If you hate the thought of working weekends or late at night, then you either need to revise your mindset, or your career plans.

Can you have it all? The rewarding career, close family, optimal health, beautiful home, robust finances, fulfilling friendships, and enriching spiritual and intellectual life that you crave? Maybe. Let's hope so. But you almost certainly can't have it all at once. When your personal vision of success rests on a perfectly balanced combination of all these things, you'll never feel successful (or very happy) at all.

Successful creative work—and successful living in general—requires self-awareness, patience, and grace. Focus your attention on the two or three elements that are most important to you right now, and accept that the best is yet to come.

HOW TO TAKE HOLIDAYS WHEN YOU'RE SELF-EMPLOYED

Whatever calibration of working and non-working hours you settle on (for now), be sure to incorporate regular rest periods into your bigger life plan. Don't let cultural and societal pressure make you feel as if you don't deserve or need to take proper breaks from your work. You do, and you must. You just need to figure out how.

When you're running a business or working for yourself, taking real time off can feel financially and logistically impossible, but it's all a matter of perspective and adjustment. Here are some general guidelines for making your time off work for you.

WORK WHEN OTHERS AREN'T WORKING

If you struggle to feel as if you're ever sufficiently "on top" of your workload to have some time out, consider taking advantage of periods when most people go off grid and the influx of emails, calls, and meetings inevitably slows. Sundays, public holidays, evenings, early mornings … all these times offer the calm and quiet to get stuff done. If you're happy to power through most of the Christmas and New Year's break, for example, you can buy yourself enough time to take a break in early January when everyone else sleepily goes back to work (and flight prices dip!).

TAKE SHORTER BREAKS, MORE FREQUENTLY

Very few freelancers have the luxury of being able to afford a two-week holiday in either the financial or professional sense—but the joy of being self-employed means you don't have to. Instead of blocking off two full weeks in the manner of a sunshine-starved 9-to-5er, break up your time off into smaller chunks: a long weekend here, a night at a hotel there (doing this means you can capitalize on last-minute deals and hotel rates which will save you money, too). Don't discount the power of the long weekend: It's amazing how rejuvenating just a few days away from home can be for the body and mind.

GIVE YOURSELF 20

As much as I'd like to advocate going totally offline for a week, for most freelancers this just isn't feasible (or even enjoyable—the stress of imagining your overflowing inbox negates the relaxation factor). Manage the influx by giving yourself 20 minutes each morning to review email and respond to any urgent requests. But leave that "Out of Office" on!

TAKE A COMPANY RETREAT

When you work for yourself and love your work, sometimes you don't actually want to take time off. Even so, it's worth taking the occasional step back from the admin and distractions that can consume daily working life. If you don't feel comfortable lying around on a beach for a week, consider the benefits of taking a company retreat (for one). Pick somewhere laidback and tranquil, take your notebook, and spend a few days regrouping and strategizing for the year ahead. Just don't forget to factor in some proper relaxation time, too.

BABIES, ETC.

It's stating the obvious to say that motherhood is one of the most transformative experiences a woman can have in her lifetime, and that experience is far too broad and variable and complex to detail here. Needless to say, the decision to become a mother is one that comes with myriad financial, physical, and emotional consequences, not least when it comes to your career.

Unfortunately, there's a shameful lack of support for working mothers at every point in the economic spectrum and in most parts of the globe. Childcare, maternity leave, and government support are still woefully underdeveloped in many countries, and entirely lacking in others, and this is before we begin to factor in the societal pressures women face to be perfect mothers, wives, and workers: to keep their children immaculately dressed and behaved while they strive to drop the "baby weight" and get straight back to work.

There's no denying that balancing motherhood and a career is not an easy task. But difficult doesn't mean impossible: millions of working mothers around the world are proof of that. Self-employment (with its lack of stable income and paid maternity leave) presents an additional challenge, but some women can attest that it's the most flexible way to find a balance that's right for you.

Sabrina De Sousa

CO-FOUNDER, DIMES

The restaurant owner and furniture designer on wholesome eating, organic growth, and the difference between working and not working

HOMETOWN
Newark, NJ

**CURRENT
LOCATION**
New York, NY

EDUCATION
School of Life (an uncompleted Bachelor's—Hunter College, NY)

EXPERIENCE
• Window Display Assistant
• Restaurant Management, Lovely Day, NY
• Furniture Studio Design Manager

DIMES STARTED OUT AS A TINY LITTLE NOOK IN CHINATOWN. Six tables. We opened this little space because we thought, "Well, we can take a risk here. It's small enough that we can really just be true to our voice."

THE GROWTH WAS REALLY ORGANIC. When we outgrew the original space, we moved across the street and turned into a full restaurant. Now the original Dimes is the deli and there's also a market next door. The market really allows people to see what we're about and where we source from.

ALISSA, MY PARTNER AT DIMES, AND I HAVE WORKED TOGETHER IN RESTAURANTS FOR OVER 10 YEARS. When we opened Dimes, we knew there was a void in the city. There just weren't really any options in New York for clean, healthy food—market-driven and vegetable-driven, of course. We knew it had to be accessible, the kind of place you could eat every day.

WE JUST WANTED TO OFFER A CLEAN, SIMPLE MENU FOR WOMEN. As women, we're very aware of what we put into our bodies, sometimes to our detriment. It's important for women to know that you can have fun with what you're eating, and it should be delicious and tasteful. You don't really have to compromise too much in order to feel wholesome and to look great.

I'VE WORKED IN RESTAURANTS WHERE THEY MASK FLAVORS WITH FAT AND YOU DON'T ACTUALLY KNOW WHAT YOU'RE EATING. THERE ISN'T A SENSE OF TRUST. And that's what was so important for Dimes. We wanted to make sure that everyone knew they could trust us, and they knew where we were sourcing, and what we were layering dishes with. Our staff have the same values. To me that's a reflection that we're doing something right.

AS A KID, MY DIET WAS VERY HIGHBROW/ LOWBROW. Both my parents are Brazilian, so there were a lot of fruits and vegetables. My mother would always make a green juice before we went to school, but also we would have Entenmann's powdered doughnuts as a snack, you know?!

THAT WAY OF EATING PLAYS INTO OUR PHILOSOPHY AT DIMES, AS WELL. You shouldn't have to really compromise all the things that make you happy, so long as you can balance the good with the not-so-good. I have a pretty weak immune system, so I've always been really fascinated with herbs and their medicinal properties and things like that.

DURING YEAR ONE OF THE BUSINESS, MY PERSONAL HEALTH DID NOT EXIST. It was a huge learning curve for Alissa and me. We spent a lot of time in our tiny bathroom, holding each other and crying because we were so overwhelmed.

PEOPLE SAY THAT STARTING A BUSINESS WITH A FRIEND IS A BAD IDEA, BUT OUR EXPERIENCE HAS BEEN THE COMPLETE OPPOSITE. Alissa and I have such symbiotic energy with each other; we really have each other's backs. She recently became a mother and has been so incredibly strong. She's taught me that I can have that in my life once I'm ready for it. That's very empowering.

BALANCE IS KNOWING THE DIFFERENCE BETWEEN WORKING AND NOT WORKING. I can't help but go out and feel inspired by something that relates to Dimes, but I *can* let go of all the fingerprints I put into the business and put faith in other people.

THERE WAS A POINT LAST YEAR WHEN I WASN'T REALLY OPEN TO NEW ENERGY IN MY LIFE AND I REALIZED I NEEDED TO BE. I thought: I can easily be this careerist woman that doesn't really think about these other facets of my life that are just as important for me to create this symbiotic happiness that I need to be me.

NOW, I UNDERSTAND THAT I CAN TAKE A STEP BACK FROM THE DAY-TO-DAY OPERATIONS AND DIMES WILL STILL DO THE MAGIC THAT IT'S SUPPOSED TO WITHOUT ME. I have to open myself up to the magic that I'm supposed to do on a personal level.

I'M AT MY HAPPIEST WHEN I'M FEELING INDUSTRIOUS. But you can lose your identity to work, and life isn't just about that. It's about making sure that you have time for your friends, have time to really enjoy the food that you're eating and chew it and shit! It's the little things.

Now, I understand that I can take a step back from the day-to-day operations and Dimes will still do the magic that it's supposed to without me. I have to open myself up to the magic that I'm supposed to do on a personal level.

Krissy Jones / Chloe Kernaghan

CO-FOUNDERS, SKY TING YOGA

The yoga instructors and studio owners on trusting your gut and keeping each other in check

HOMETOWN
KJ: Portage, IN
CK: Asan, GU

EDUCATION
KJ: Bachelor of Science in Kinesiology—Indiana University
CK: Bachelor of Fine Arts—New York University

CURRENT LOCATION
BOTH:
New York, NY

EXPERIENCE
KJ:
• Nike Trainer
• Freelance dancer, choreographer, and yoga instructor

CK:
• Maître d'
• Freelance choreographer and yoga teacher

KJ: SKY TING IS A YOGA STUDIO IN NEW YORK THAT CHLOE AND I OPENED IN 2015. We had a specific vision for a new yoga studio, one that was not in New York City already, someplace that we would love practicing in, that's light and bright and kind of authentic to our demographic and vibe.

CK: KRISSY AND I BOTH GREW UP DANCING. When we started practicing yoga, it all made sense. It keeps us in our bodies, but also engages with an esoteric dialogue that we were both drawn towards. When we moved to NYC separately, we knew that office jobs didn't make sense for either of us. We wanted to marry our desire to be present in our physical space with making a living. Yoga was the answer to that.

KJ: IT WAS REALLY MAGICAL AS WELL THE WAY THIS STUDIO CAME INTO OUR HANDS. On New Year's Eve 2014, I was like, "Hey, I think I want to open up a yoga studio maybe this year." And then a month later my boyfriend was looking on Craigslist and he actually knew the landlord from years back. So he just called him and the landlord was like, "Hey yeah, I love yoga, I'd love to have yoga in my building, what great energy!" I was really dragging my feet. But then the landlord called me and was basically like, "Now or never." So I closed my eyes and signed the lease.

KJ: THE YOGA THAT WE TEACH AT SKY TING IS VERY PRACTICAL AND TECHNICAL. It's less about religion and more about useful skills that you can have to enhance your life, and we really teach yoga for longevity and wellbeing instead of fitness. So that's what kind of sets us apart.

KJ: SKY TING HAS GROWN SO QUICKLY SINCE WE OPENED. We've opened a second studio and launched a teacher training course. When I signed the first lease, we didn't even have a business plan. That all came after. It's so crazy in retrospect. I thank God it happened the way it did because I just took a risk and I knew that I had a vision; I knew that this space was perfect for yoga and I didn't want to give that up.

CK: A LOT OF IT WAS ABOUT TRUSTING OUR GUTS. We knew we could trust the practice—the material's there, it's magic in and of itself. For us, it was about seeing that the universe was giving us all these opportunities in a row, and being able to trust in those signals.

KJ: TAKE RISKS WHILE YOU CAN AND ASK PEOPLE FOR HELP. You would be so surprised, especially when you are doing something that is good for society: People want to help. I want to help people, help the community, have tools [for people] to be well in their lives.

KJ: I MANAGE A LOT OF PEOPLE NOW. That's the hardest thing for me in doing this—being a good boss and being a leader and having tough conversations that are sometimes awkward that I don't want to have. But I have to. I just have to suck it up and try to be as graceful and kind as I can.

KJ: WE WORK VERY SOCIALLY–MY JOB IS ESSENTIALLY PUBLIC SPEAKING AND BEING WITH PEOPLE ALL THE TIME. So when I go home I do an inward practice. If I don't do that I feel crazy and frazzled and not very stable.

CK: KRISSY AND I KEEP EACH OTHER IN CHECK ALL THE TIME. I'll be like, "Hey! Go sit in a plow for 20 minutes and cool off!" It's all about checks and balances, and feeling good.

KJ: YOGA SHOULDN'T BE COMPLICATED, AND IT DOESN'T HAVE TO BE DOGMATIC. You can really incorporate five minutes of this stuff into your day and feel a lot different. That's the whole goal: to transform and be better every day, in every moment.

KJ: THE REAL CRUX OF MY MISSION IS JUST TO HAVE A NICE LIFE, AND TO INSPIRE OTHERS TO BE THEIR MOST BADASS SELVES. The most powerful, kind people that they can be. I'm not really looking for the end goal, I'm just having a lot of fun and it feels really authentic and the right thing I should be doing now. Feeling kind and abundant and nice to people … that's my definition of success.

CK: I AGREE. WE'RE NOT NECESSARILY LOOKING TO BE A SUPER-LUCRATIVE BUSINESS; WE REALLY JUST HAVE SOME GOOD TOOLS THAT WE WANT TO SHARE. At the end of the day, it's all about the feedback system. When we hear that the work has been transformative for a student, it's like, "Oh, OK. This is working!"

Neneh Cherry

MUSICIAN

The iconic singer-songwriter on raising daughters, protecting your inner sanctum, and motherhood as destiny

HOMETOWN
Stockholm, Sweden

CURRENT LOCATION
London, UK

EDUCATION
Life

EXPERIENCE
• Mother
• Singer
• Songwriter

I FIRST CAME TO LONDON WHEN I WAS 16. I went to visit my friend Ari, who was the lead singer of The Slits, and just ended up staying. Being around [The Slits members] Tessa Pollitt, Viv Albertine, and Ari was hugely influential. They were three extraordinary women, doing something I'd never seen or heard before.

I WENT OUT INTO THE WORLD AT A REALLY YOUNG AGE, WITH THE FULL SUPPORT OF MY PARENTS. I learned a few lessons the really fucking hard way.

I'D BEEN LIVING IN NEW YORK, SO WHEN I CAME TO LONDON I FELT COCKSURE. I thought London was this little pussycat compared to the big tiger of New York. I ended up being attacked by a man in Battersea when I was 16 and walking back from the store. It was a hugely disturbing, awful thing that has affected my entire life. I decided, very consciously, that it wasn't going to kill my spirit. So I just picked myself up and carried on.

IN LONDON, I DISCOVERED THIS ENERGY THAT WAS FREE, VERY CREATIVE, AND ALL ABOUT STRETCHING OUT AND PUSHING BEYOND YOUR OWN LIMITATIONS. Taking risks was something everyone was trying to do: It was OK to get inside whatever it was you were trying to say. When I went in the studio to record the first Rip Rig + Panic album, I'd never sung and didn't really know what I was doing. But as soon as I heard the music, I felt OK.

MY BEST FRIEND ANDREA AND I USED TO GO OUT AND JUST DANCE. We'd take our shoes off, tuck our skirts into our knickers, and dance until we dropped! That was when we went to church and said our prayers.

FOR A LOT OF PEOPLE, [MY FIRST ALBUM] *RAW LIKE SUSHI* REPRESENTED SOMETHING VERY STYLIZED. But when I think about where I was in myself at that time, that wasn't what we were trying to do. The way the music sounded, and the way I was dressed—it all felt like a very important part of what we were trying to say. It was not just about being rebellious—although that was an important part of the overall statement.

CONFIDENCE IS SOMETHING I'VE ALWAYS EXPERIENCED IN MOMENTS. I've had these spells of time throughout my life, where I'm like: "OK, right now: I wish I could feel like this all the time." But life isn't like that.

CONFIDENCE ISN'T ABOUT BEING LOUD AND BALLSY. It's also about caressing your vulnerability. I remember, when I was younger, feeling quite proud of the fact that I didn't allow myself to feel intimidated by the things I was supposed to be intimidated by. That isn't to say that I wasn't insecure, but I decided to wear a hat—metaphorically, and often physically!

AS A WOMAN, I'VE ALWAYS LIKED WEARING GREAT SHOES AND HATS. Jewelry, too. Wearing the right shoes really affects how you feel when you're doing your job. [Stylist] Judy Blame and I were trying to make our own style, and that's really one of the things that has always interested me the most. It all helped me feel a bit more hardcore when I needed to be hardcore.

I FEEL BLESSED THAT I HAVE ALWAYS BEEN PART OF A FAMILY OF VERY INTERESTING THINKERS AND STRONG SPIRITS. My mother was an artist who worked on a lot of different levels. Growing up with her and the women that were her friends has also been a big thing. Since she passed, I've become really great friends with a lot of her friends, and so have my daughters Naima, Tyson, and Mabel. In a way, my mother's friends were my pioneers. Our pioneers. They've definitely given me so much, there's no doubt about it.

I KNEW I WANTED TO HAVE KIDS BY THE TIME I WAS 17. That was in my karma, and it was kind of the thing that came first. Naima came when I was 18 years old. I just picked her up and took her with me, and knew we were going to be fine. I had this idea of what I needed to do and what I wanted to do and I thought: So long as I'm consistent with her, why shouldn't she be able to be anywhere with me?

MY DAUGHTER NAIMA CAME ON TOUR WITH ME WHEN SHE WAS SIX OR SEVEN WEEKS OLD. I just made it work. The tour manager had kids (thank God!) and he wore her in a sling when I was on stage. I gave her a bath at the same time every night. I had milk in my breast. She sat with me the rest of the time, and we were fine.

THE REALITY OF ME BEING A MOTHER WAS ALWAYS THERE. It's always been a part of everything. It's the thing that makes *me* make sense. I would never say to someone: "You should have kids, it will make it you complete." Everyone has a different journey. But it was always my journey; the route I was meant to take.

FAMILY HAS ALWAYS BEEN AN INNER SANCTUM AND THE PLACE WHERE EVERYTHING STARTS FOR ME. I still go and sit on my bed when I want to start writing songs.

THESE DAYS, IT'S ALMOST HIP TO BE A MOTHER WHO WORKS, AND HAS A PERFECT FAMILY AND KIDS. You're supposed to be able to go and lie down, have a child naturally, and then be perfectly fit and back at work within a few months. I look around sometimes and it really stresses me out. I want to tell women to cherish the moment, relax, chill, remember that they look beautiful! As women, we put so much pressure on ourselves. We can look at our voluptuous friends and think they're beautiful and sensual, and then fucking hate everything about our own bodies.

WHEN "BUFFALO STANCE" CAME OUT, I WAS THE SKINNIEST I'VE EVER BEEN IN MY LIFE. But I remember at the time feeling that I was big. Now, I look at pictures and I'm like, "Shit girl. There was nothing on you!" At the time, I thought my ass was huge.

ALL THAT BODY IMAGE STUFF RUNS SO DEEP, AND I RESENT IT SO MUCH. I look at my daughters being consumed by the same worries and wonder if it's actually gotten worse. The media is so much more forceful now. But even though we're all still affected by these same body-image and confidence issues, I can feel a positive, DIY wave of energy coming through: that feeling of "I can make a change" by working, or developing your own little idea.

MY YOUNGEST DAUGHTER AND HER FRIENDS ARE REALLY FULL-ON FEMINISTS. Even her boyfriend is a feminist. So beneath all this synthetic, over-processed stuff, there are a lot of great things happening. Sometimes, we have to hit that point of desperation before we really start to change things.

THE PUNK AND HIP-HOP SCENES THAT I CAME OUT OF WERE VERY POLITICAL IN A SIMILAR WAY. Even though we weren't shouting politics as individuals it was very much about the political and the social. When I look back at the clothes I chose to wear, we thought about it and we worked on it and we had a lot of fun with it, because we were in a way, yes, making a statement. But it was a statement that was very much coming from our hearts.

WE ALWAYS PROTECTED OUR SHIT. I signed to Circa Records because it was smaller and gave us more creative freedom, but we've always run stuff out of the house, for better or for worse.

FAMILY HAS ALWAYS BEEN THE CORE. The office was always in the house. We had a studio at home, and that was a conscious decision: The think tank was always ours. We kept control of the videos, the visuals, the sounds, the music, the whole thing. We hopefully weren't obsessive, but we also weren't going to let any of it go.

ON THE RARE OCCASION THAT WE DID ALLOW OTHER PEOPLE TO TALK US INTO DOING THINGS, IT WAS JUST A JOKE. They watered it down and made it shit.

IF YOU STICK TO YOUR GUNS, YOU MIGHT NOT GET PAID SO WELL, BUT WHO KNOWS? SOMETIMES YOU MIGHT GET PAID MORE. I think that's what we did, with "Buffalo Stance." We just didn't go with the people who didn't fucking get it. It wasn't going to work any other way.

THE MAINSTREAM MUSIC INDUSTRY IS THIS AGE-OBSESSED ENVIRONMENT WHERE YOU'RE OLD IF YOU'RE OVER 25. You can be 33 if you're really, really, really famous, and you can be 65 if you're Mick Jagger-famous. I like the place where I am; it's a kinder world. The leftfield is a more patient, tolerant, interesting place. I feel like I belong there.

In a sense, I felt the same way when I was 25. I was like: I'm here, I'm pregnant, I'm Swedish, I'm African, I'm from New York. I'm hip-hop. I'm punk. I'm weird. I'm whatever. You have to know what you're about and celebrate it. Fuck standing up there feeling shit about it. Take it, love it—or don't do it.

IN MY TEENS AND EARLY TWENTIES, I COULD FEEL ALL OF THE POSSIBILITIES AND DREAMS FLOATING AROUND MY HEAD. They're still there, but I'm starting to reach a place where I'm better at understanding what it is I'm about. I'm looking ahead and feeling like I'm starting to reach the places that I always want to get to. That's incredibly exciting.

RIGHT NOW, I'M IN A REALLY HAPPY PLACE. I feel really inspired. I'm on one of those thresholds in life that kind of send you off into a new era … I'm a mother, I'm a grandmother, I'm a woman. I feel young, I feel old, depending where I am on any given day. That's how I do it. That's how I roll. It feels good to know that that's OK.

IN A SENSE, I FELT THE SAME WAY WHEN I WAS 25. I was like: I'm here, I'm pregnant, I'm Swedish, I'm African, I'm from New York. I'm hip-hop. I'm punk. I'm weird. I'm whatever. You have to know what you're about and celebrate it. Fuck standing up there feeling shit about it. Take it, love it—or don't do it.

OUTRO

WORKING IT OUT
A Few Final Thoughts

For most of human history, work was something people did because they had to (or were forced to), with little expectation beyond generating the means to provide shelter and basic sustenance for themselves and their families. For many people, especially women, this reality endures.

If you're reading this book, you're probably one of the lucky ones—a human being who is fortunate enough to be able to think about work in a different, far more expansive context: Work as passion. Work as vocation. Work as pleasure. Work as purpose.

Whatever your perspective, the pursuit of a happy and healthy working life is one of the most important journeys you'll ever undertake. You'll probably spend a great proportion of your lifetime at work, and you owe it to yourself to try to get it right.

Try, along the way, to enjoy each stage for what it is. To be grateful for the chance to create a career of meaning and beauty. To find joy in the task, despite how mundane it might seem. And, above all, try to stay patient with yourself while you figure it all out.

When it comes down to it, it's this—the "figuring it out" part—that really makes up a life's work.

I wish you all the success and joy in the world with your own!

Phoebe

RESOURCES
Further Reading and Research

WEBSITES

THEWWCLUB.COM
Articles, worksheets, event information, and interviews from The Working Women's Club (that's us!).

NYTIMES.COM
Quite possibly the best newspaper in the world, with the business, finance, travel, and wellness advice to match.

THEPARISREVIEW.ORG
The iconic literary magazine's site is packed with fabulous interviews.

HBR.ORG
Needless to say, *Harvard Business Review* has some smart things to say about work and business.

THEGUARDIAN.COM/CAREERS
The British newspaper's dedicated job section is full of great tips and interviews.

THESCHOOLOFLIFE.COM
Alain de Botton's guide to navigating modern life. Events, videos, and workshops in a city near you.

THEBOOKOFLIFE.ORG
An ever-growing online bible of wisdom for work, life, and love. The online content counterpart to The School of Life's IRL events (see above).

ITSNICETHAT.COM
This London-based studio and site has a keen eye for emerging creative talent.

INTOTHEGLOSS.COM/SECTIONS/INTERVIEWS
Great career advice (and even better skincare tips) from a plethora of fashion and beauty industry insiders.

99U.COM
Practical, actionable advice for all aspects of your creative career.

INC.COM
A great resource of articles and advice for small business owners.

FORBES.COM
Business, tech, and finance news in one big place (and, of course, those famous lists).

ZENHABITS.NET
Fresh and soothing advice for mindful entrepreneurship and living.

COVETEUR.COM/SUPERTAGS/CAREER
Primarily an online style destination—but one with a great archive of career articles.

ROOKIEMAG.COM
Awesome reading material for the young and young-at-heart.

SETHGODIN.COM
A forever thought-provoking blog

from one of the world's foremost marketing gurus.

PODCASTS

MAKE IT WORK—THE WW CLUB
My interviews with insightful working women worldwide.

HOW I BUILT THIS—NPR
Inspiring stories from innovators and entrepreneurs.

THE ENTREPRENEURS AND *THE BIG INTERVIEW*—MONOCLE
Two shows, both with great guests, from the London-based business and lifestyle magazine.

DESERT ISLAND DISCS—
BBC RADIO 4
Decades of timeless interviews with some of the world's most fascinating people.

LONGFORM PODCAST—
LONGFORM.ORG
Thorough, in-depth Q&A sessions with some of America's very best journalists and writers.

STARTUP—GIMLET MEDIA
An expertly-produced podcast about what it's really like to get a business off the ground.

OH BOY—MAN REPELLER
A smart, creative man interviews a whole host of smart, creative women.

ADVICE SITES AND BUREAUS

STUDENTAID.ED.GOV/SA
Solid advice on repaying your student loans for US graduates.

MONEYSUPERMARKET.COM
Tips on ways to save money on everything from car insurance to credit card bills.

SCORE.ORG
Tons of free advice for small business owners in the US.

BONDSTREET.COM
Financing and free advice for independent entrepreneurs.

PRINCES-TRUST.ORG.UK
An incredible resource of support and funding for 18-to-30-year-olds wanting to turn their big ideas into businesses in the UK.

TOOLS AND APPS

EVERNOTE / evernote.com
Simply the best digital notebook in the game.

DROPBOX / dropbox.com
A great way to secure and organize your files in the cloud.

GSUITE / gsuite.google.com
A comprehensive suite of easy-to-use business tools and apps from Google.

SQUARESPACE / squarespace.com
The best, most intuitive platform for creating a slick online portfolio.

SLACK / slack.com
A simple, highly effective way to communicate with your team.

NOISLI / noisli.com
A great "white noise" sound for freelancers working in noisy coffee shops.

MONEY MANAGEMENT

MINT / mint.com
Stay on top of your incomings, outgoings, budgets, and financial charges. Knowledge is power.

ONTREES / ontrees.com
Simple tools for making the most of your money. Mint for Brits.

ROBINHOOD / robinhood.com
Free stock trading for beginners.

ACORNS / acorns.com
A genius app that automatically invests your spare change.

ELLEVEST / ellevest.com
An investment platform built for and by women.

WORKSPACES
LONDON

COUNTER ALBION—SHOREDITCH
albion-uk.london/counteralbion
A spacious and airy workspace with great lunch options and a life-changing breakfast buffet.

ACE HOTEL—SHOREDITCH
acehotel.com/london
Forever packed, but nice and cozy for a grey London day. Get there early and bunker down.

GOOGLE CAMPUS—OLD STREET
campus.co/london/en
You have to be a member to use this great coworking space, but membership is free. Win win.

NEWINGTON TABLE—
NEWINGTON GREEN
newingtontable.co.uk
Delicious breakfasts and a calm, park-side setting. Get the oat milk cappuccino.

NEW YORK

ST COFFEE @ SINCERELY, TOMMY—BEDFORD-STUYVESANT
sincerelytommy.com/pages/cafe
Get some work done at the marble coffee counter, and pick up some beautiful clothes while you're at it.

ANNEX—FORT GREENE
greenegrape.com/annex
This Fort Greene favorite can get busy, but it's good when you're in the mood for a buzzy vibe.

STONE FRUIT ESPRESSO—BEDFORD-STUYVESANT
stonefruitespresso.com
A verdant, airy space with delicious healthy lunch options.

SPREADHOUSE CAFE—LOWER EAST SIDE

spreadhouse.com
It can be hard (impossible?) to find space, outlets, and a freelancer-friendly vibe in downtown Manhattan. Spreadhouse delivers.

MCNALLY JACKSON—SOHO
mcnallyjackson.com
A great place to do some research (aka reading expensive magazines for free).

WHYNOT COFFEE—LOWER EAST SIDE
facebook.com/whynotcoffeenyc
A cute little coffee shop that turns into a gallery by night. Music is on point, too.

STUMPTOWN COFFEE ROASTERS—GREENWICH VILLAGE
yelp.com/biz/stumptown-new-york
Good, strong coffee and a nice location near Washington Square Park.

LOS ANGELES

GO GET EM TIGER—LARCHMONT VILLAGE
gandb.coffee/gget
Almond and macadamia milk lattes. Enough said.

DINOSAUR COFFEE—SILVER LAKE
dinosaurcoffee.com
The neon-lit tagline for this airy coffee shop is "Things Will Be Fine." Yes, indeed.

BRU—LOS FELIZ
brucoffeebar.com
There are no outlets here, but that can be quite nice—race against your laptop battery or do some "analogue" work.

THE SPRINGS—DOWNTOWN L.A.
thespringsla.com
Do a yoga class, get a colonic (!) and get some work done, all in one gorgeous place.

WANDERLUST HOLLYWOOD—HOLLYWOOD

wanderlusthollywood.com
Nutritious L.A.-style fare and a
lovely terrace setting.

ARCHIVES AND LIBRARIES
LONDON
THE BRITISH LIBRARY—EUSTON
bl.uk
Every single book ever published.
Totally silent reading rooms. A
new Business and IP Centre that
even has a (female) entrepreneur
in residence. What more could you
want/need?

NEW YORK
THE NEW YORK PUBLIC LIBRARY—
VARIOUS
nypl.org
There are numerous NYPL locations
dotted across New York. For
workspace wow factor, you can't
beat the newly reopened Rose
Reading Room.

THE INTERNATIONAL CENTER OF
PHOTOGRAPHY LIBRARY—MIDTOWN
icp.org/facilities/library
An extensive collection of
photobooks and other resources.

THE FASHION INSTITUTE
OF TECHNOLOGY LIBRARY—
CHELSEA
fitnyc.edu/library
Fashion magazine back issues,
show DVDs, books, trend forecasts,
and more (accessible to researchers
by appointment only).

LOS ANGELES
WEST HOLLYWOOD LIBRARY—
WEST HOLLYWOOD
colapublib.org/libs/whollywood
This is bright, light, and offers
three hours of free parking. There's
also a nice lawn outside for your
lunch break.

CENTRAL LIBRARY—DOWNTOWN
lapl.org/branches/central-library
You can't park here, so take the
Metro/Uber instead and enjoy

a few tranquil hours in the
rotunda cafe.

OFFICE GOODS
SMYTHSON—LONDON (VARIOUS)
smythson.com
Treat yourself to a personalized
notebook for the ultimate in
to-do listing.

GOODS FOR THE STUDY—
NOLITA, NEW YORK
goodsforthestudy.
mcnallyjacksonstore.com
A boutique treasure trove of
beautiful objects and tools for
the office.

POKETO—DOWNTOWN
LOS ANGELES
poketo.com
Colorful art and design objects
that will brighten up your daily
working life.

MOLESKINE
moleskine.com
Makers of some of the very
best notebooks and planners in
the world.

MUJI
Muji.com
Stationery and storage heaven.

FURTHER READING
ANYTHING BY ALAIN
DE BOTTON
The philosopher-entrepreneur is
behind some of the best work-
focused titles of our times. Try
Status Anxiety and *The Pleasures
and Sorrows of Work* to begin.

HOW TO SERIES FROM THE
SCHOOL OF LIFE
De Botton's business The School of
Life produces guides to a number
of contemporary dilemmas and
quandaries. Try *How to Find
Fulfilling Work* by Roman Krznaric as
a starting point.

DO THE WORK BY
STEVEN PRESSFIELD
A tough-love handbook will help
you push through any and every
creative rut.

*MAKE YOUR MARK / MANAGE YOUR
DAY-TO-DAY / MAXIMIZE YOUR
POTENTIAL* BY 99U
Three separate titles jam-packed
with stellar advice for creative
professionals.

*THE INDEX CARD: WHY PERSONAL
FINANCE DOESN'T HAVE TO BE
COMPLICATED* BY HELAINE OLEN
Does what it says on the tin.
Clear and simple money stuff you
must know.

*BIG MAGIC: CREATIVE LIVING
BEYOND FEAR* BY ELIZABETH
GILBERT
The bestselling author shares some
genuinely inspiring advice for living
a creative life.

*THE LIFE-CHANGING MAGIC OF
TIDYING UP* BY MARIE KONDO
Not technically a career book, but
one that will help you to streamline
your surroundings and your mind in
the process.

FLOW BY MIHALY CSIKSZENTMIHALYI
The Hungarian psychologist
breaks down his game-changing
theory on the state of optimal
creative satisfaction.

AUTHOR BIOGRAPHY

Phoebe Lovatt

**JOURNALIST, MODERATOR, AND FOUNDER OF
THE WW CLUB**

HOMETOWN
London, UK

**CURRENT
LOCATION**
New York, NY

EDUCATION
BA Hons, History—University College London

EXPERIENCE
• Founding Editor, House Seven
• Freelance Contributor at *Dazed, Elle, i-D, GQ,* and
  The Guardian
• Columnist at *Courier*

Phoebe Lovatt is a journalist, moderator, and the founder of
The WW Club, a community and resource for working women
worldwide. Born and raised in London, Phoebe started her
career as a freelance features writer for publications including
Dazed, Elle, and *GQ,* and was the founding editor of Soho House's
digital platform, House Seven. Since launching The WW Club in
her former base of Los Angeles in 2015, she has hosted career-
focused events in cities from Paris to Taipei and partnered with
Nike Women, Topshop, and DKNY. She now runs the club from
her current home, New York City, and continues to write about
women in business, city life, and the changing world of work.

ACKNOWLEDGMENTS

Many thanks to Ali, Geoff, Martha, and everyone at Prestel, for making all of this possible.

This book is dedicated to the women who have shaped my life.

To Molly and Ellie, my original girl gang and surrogate sisters. To Maire and Anne, my super-stylish and smart surrogate aunts.

To Grace, Jenny, Suz, Sharma, ZJ, Scarlett, Charlotte, Naomi, and all my amazing friends in London, who make me so grateful to call that city home.

To the women in Los Angeles who believed in me in the earliest days of The WW Club. To the women in New York who make me proud to hustle among them now.

To Madeline and Alicia for helping me to stay sane in Suite 701, where this project slowly but surely came to life.

To Jane, Sarah, Charlotte, and Louise, for the advice and support from the earliest days of my career. To Hattie, who gave me my first commission.

To the brilliant and inspiring women featured on these pages, who so generously shared their time and hard-earned insights.

To the women who follow and support The WW Club worldwide. Connecting with you has been the most rewarding experience of my professional life.

To my International Girl Crew—you know who you are!—who continuously inspire me to up the levels, on every level.

To Alison, my real-life fairy godmother, for giving the very best advice. To my grandmothers Molly, whose work ethic is unparalleled, and Rosemarie, who has always encouraged me to live life on my own terms. To Margaret, who was loved and is missed.

And to my mother Jane, above all. Thank you for instilling me with an ability to laugh at almost anything, an endless appetite to experience the world, and (hopefully) some semblance of your independence, compassion, and calm. I love you.

© Prestel Verlag, Munich • London • New York, 2017
A member of Verlagsgruppe Random House GmbH
Neumarkter Strasse 28 · 81673 Munich

In respect to links in the book, Verlagsgruppe
Random House expressly notes that no illegal
content was discernible on the linked sites at the
time the links were created. The Publisher has no
influence at all over the current and future design,
content or authorship of the linked sites. For this
reason Verlagsgruppe Random House expressly
disassociates itself from all content on linked sites
that has been altered since the link was created and
assumes no liability for such content.

© for the text by Phoebe Lovatt

Prestel Publishing Ltd.
14–17 Wells Street
London W1T 3PD

Prestel Publishing
900 Broadway, Suite 603
New York, NY 10003

Library of Congress Control Number: 2017940315
A CIP catalogue record for this book is available from
the British Library.

Editorial direction: Ali Gitlow
Copyediting and proofreading: Martha Jay
Design and layout: The Studio of Williamson Curran
Production management: Friederike Schirge
Separations: Reproline Mediateam
Printing and binding: TBB, a.s. Banská Bystrica
Paper: Tauro

Verlagsgruppe Random House FSC® N001967

Printed in Slovakia

ISBN 978-3-7913-8314-9

www.prestel.com

All photographs © the individual subjects.

All icons from thenounproject.com. Intro:
"Play" icon by Nice and Serious; The Legwork:
"Dumbbell" icon by Andrey; Work It!: "Speaker"
icon by Korokoro; Make It Work: "Diamond"
icon by Numero Uno; Work Well: "Bulb" icon by
mikicon; Working on 100: "Battery" icon by Nancy;
Outro: "Stop" icon by Shastry; p. 1, p. 59, p. 151:
"Pencil" icon by Anastasia Latysheva; p. 142, p. 145:
"Question mark" icon by unlimicon.